SCHIZOPHRENIA
AND
BIPOLAR DISORDERS

often misdiagnosed

often mistreated

A Family Manual

Schizophrenia

and

Bipolar Disorders

often misdiagnosed

often mistreated

A Family Manual

HERBERT WAGEMAKER, M.D.

with Ann Buchholz

Schizophrenia and Bipolar Disorders
often misdiagnosed, often mistreated
A Family Manual

Requests for information should be addressed to:
H. Wagemaker, M.D.
Ponte Vedra Publishers
P.O. Box 773
Ponte Vedra Beach, FL 32004-0773

Library of Congress Cataloging-in-Publication Data

Wagemaker, Herbert
Schizophrenia and bipolar disorders — often misdiagnosed, often mistreated : A Family Manual / Herbert Wagemaker, M.D.
with Ann Buchholz
Includes bibliographical references and index.
ISBN: 0-9654996-1-8

Some of the names in this book have been changed to protect the privacy of the individuals described.

Edited by Ann Buchholz
Cover, book, and diagrams designed by Teresa St. John

Printed in the United States of America

*This book is dedicated to
my good friend and colleague*

Steven Lippmann, M.D.

Acknowledgments

This book has been a twenty-year task. It all started in Gainesville, Florida, during the early 1970s when I was in charge of the community mental health center patients who needed hospitalization. This experience sparked my interest in schizophrenia, an interest that has lasted throughout the subsequent years. I would like to acknowledge and thank the following people I have met during this period.

In Gainesville, Florida, the staff of nurses and social workers on the inpatient unit and at the community mental health center were outstanding. They taught me a lot, and together we laid the foundation of treatment that is contained in this book.

Dr. John Schwab was responsible for securing my position in the residency program at the University of Florida. He was a valued mentor both at the University of Florida and at the University of Louisville. In 1975 when he was chairman of the Department of Psychiatry at the University of Louisville, Dr. Schwab invited me to join the faculty. I became the director of the inpatient psychiatric unit affiliated with the medical school. Again I was blessed with a fine staff of social workers and nurses. These people are my all-time heroes for their dedication and compassion.

Dr. Steven Lippmann joined the faculty of the University of Louisville in the late 1970s. He brought with him good training in psychiatry and a real heart for patients suffering from mental illness, as well as commitment to the poor and neglected of our community.

Ann Buchholz provided editorial guidance on the completion of this book. Her help was invaluable.

Lisa Alberts of the National Institute of Mental Health read the book in its final stages for revision and gave me encouragement and valuable suggestions. She also contributed a unique perspective as both an objective reader and editor.

Teresa St. John designed the book cover and illustrations. She also contributed priceless assistance in the final stages of the book's presentation and production.

I am indebted to all these fine professionals. And I am grateful to my family for their support and love. I also want to thank my patients and their families. This book would not have been possible without their contributions. I am indebted to them. They shared with me their inner feelings and thoughts, which helped me understand what they were going through as they suffered the many problems associated with mental illness. I am truly grateful to them all.

Contents

Introduction

This book has been in the making a long time. I first became interested in these illnesses as a psychiatric resident in the late 1960s and early 1970s. Even at that time in my training, I felt very strongly that these were genetic illnesses. Immediately after my residency, I worked for a community mental health center in Gainesville, Florida. My patients suffered from schizophrenia or bipolar disorders. I struggled with them and their families. Too often, patients were sent to the state hospital and looked upon as chronic, hopeless cases. I learned that I could get patients out of an acute psychotic state safely and rapidly. I also learned that hospitals, especially state hospitals, were not good places for treatment. So we treated patients aggressively and got them out of the hospital as fast as we could.

I also found out that parents shouldered most of the burdens of care for their sons and daughters. Many were encumbered with a heavy load. This despondency was written on their faces, prominent in their thoughts, and central in their lives.

I felt we could treat patients better, that there was help for them. I felt we could do more for their families. I knew that community mental health centers and state hospitals could do better jobs.

Being involved in research also allowed me to be exposed to new ideas, new ways of looking at these illnesses. I saw patients do well. I watched them resume normal lives. Some of them became nurses and doctors; some of them became teachers; some got married and had children. Many are self-supporting and independent.

This book came out of my experiences. I hope that it brings encouragement and hope to many families. But more than that, I hope that it will bring to patients more accurate diagnoses

13

and better treatments, so that they can lead more normal and independent lives at work, at school, and with their families. I am confident that many families can be released from the burden of these illnesses, so that they too can have hope.

1
There is Hope

Ned was twenty-seven when he came for his first appointment. A tall, neatly-groomed young man, he sat in the chair across from my desk, and we began the initial interview. Ned was quiet, his answers brief. Some of my questions may have seemed familiar to him; this was not his first session with a psychiatrist.

At the age of twenty, Ned was diagnosed as suffering from the symptoms of schizophrenia. Over the years since then, he had dropped out of school, worked irregularly, and lost touch with friends; his life had become increasingly limited. For seven long years he had been in and out of psychiatric hospitals.

Fortunately Ned's family remained involved with him. They had moved to Florida when Ned's father retired. A family friend had referred them to me.

On the day of Ned's first appointment in my office, his parents accompanied him and sat beside him during the initial interview. They were quiet, caring parents who had stood by their son and supported him in whatever ways they were able. For seven years they had faced the uncertainty of Ned's illness and future. As I talked with them, I saw the pervasive sadness that I have seen in the eyes of so many parents whose sons or daughters have become incapacitated by devastating illness. This sadness reaches deep inside the hearts of parents who have watched the promise of their child's future dwindle. This sadness lingers when these parents no longer hold any hope, when their hope has been dashed to pieces by the daily struggles with chronic illness.

15

Ned's symptoms first started when he was a junior in college. Two weeks before Thanksgiving he started having difficulty getting to sleep. Once asleep, he often woke up in the middle of the night. He was bothered by his dreams and thoughts. He began to doubt his friends and feared they were plotting against him. When he attended classes, he believed people were staring at him. When he went to the library, he was sure people had followed him and were talking about him in the aisles. To him the world was an increasingly hostile, threatening place.

Then the voice began. Softly at first, someone called his name, but no one was there. In a short time the voice became a conversation — more than one voice and no longer soft. The voices accused him, threatened him. They yelled and argued and were with him all the time. He could not study, nor sleep. He lived in terror.

His roommate took him to the infirmary where Ned was admitted to the psychiatric unit. During the course of his hospitalization, he was treated with antipsychotic medications. In several weeks he was out of the acute phase of the illness and approaching discharge.

Ned's parents visited him regularly. Though they saw improvement, they remained deeply concerned. Their son who had once functioned normally, now was lethargic and showed little expression. His fingers trembled; his arms and shoulders were stiff.

The psychiatrist had told them Ned had the symptoms of schizophrenia. He had also informed them that patients suffering from schizophrenia often have a hard time concentrating. Thus, going to school or holding down a job could be very stressful to them. The psychiatrist further advised that these patients have difficulty living independently, and that their relationships are rarely stable.

Ned's parents felt as if they had lost their son. They could not believe what was happening to him, and they feared what both Ned and the family would be facing in the years ahead.

After several weeks in the hospital, Ned was able to go home. He was stabilized on his antipsychotic medication. He did not hear the voices so acutely now, though they always seemed to be in the back of his mind. His paranoid thoughts had decreased, his sleep had improved, and the stiffness in his body had lessened. But he was not able to do much more than sit for hours at a time just watching television. He rarely went out and slept more and more — just withdrew from life.

During these months, his parents' heartache became an unspoken sadness they endured daily. Though some days were better than others, life seemed to plod on. For periods Ned would strive to work; once he even attempted to go back to school. Concentration was difficult; however, and he inevitably had to quit his job or drop out of classes. On several occasions, he had to be rehospitalized and restabilized on his medication.

When Ned's father retired and the family moved to Florida, they may have hoped the change could bring new possibilities for their son. On that day of Ned's first appointment with me, his parents conveyed sadness, yet I also sensed they were willing to keep searching for answers. During the interview they provided family history that included hospitalization of other family members: Ned's mother's sister had been treated and was still on medication for depression, and Ned's paternal uncle and grandfather had suffered from alcoholism. This history was unusual. Most often families who have a history of affective disorders, such as depression, bipolar disease, schizoaffective illness, or alcoholism, have offspring who suffer from the symptoms of affective disorder, not the symptoms of schizophrenia that Ned had experienced.

Could Ned have been diagnosed incorrectly? If so, what was the correct diagnosis? Everything pointed to a diagnosis of schizophrenia — everything, that is, except family history. I asked Ned's parents if he had ever been tried on lithium.

"No," they answered, and for a moment I sensed they were dubious of trying yet another medication. When I suggested a trial on lithium, however, both Ned and his parents agreed to this approach.

I started Ned on Lithium Carbonate 300 milligrams in the morning and at bedtime. The next week he returned to my office with his parents. He had tolerated lithium without any side effects. He was sleeping well. The delusional thinking and auditory hallucinations had abated — all promising developments. I followed him for another week. At our next session I reduced his antipsychotic medication by 10 milligrams. The following week the antipsychotic was reduced by another 10 milligrams; then it was decreased to 10 milligrams and finally discontinued. During this time Ned showed no signs nor symptoms of his illness. He reported feeling better; he was getting out more, doing things. Four weeks later he had a job in a 7-11 store. He began to smile more often. Hope returned to his future and to the eyes of his parents.

After three months on the job, Ned made plans to go back to school, to finish what he started ten years ago. His thoughts had cleared, and the paranoia and the voices had disappeared. For the first time in years, Ned saw a future, a direction, and he had the motivation and energy to embark on that pathway.

His parents are amazed by this turnaround. For the first time, the long years of uncertainty and sadness seem part of the past. A year and a half later, at Christmas, they came with Ned for his appointment. "We have our son back," his mother exulted, "What a great Christmas present."

Though this story has a happy ending, I want to emphasize again that it has been a poignant story — seven years of wasted life, seven years of disappointment. And this tragedy has occurred repeatedly in the lives of other patients who like Ned have been diagnosed as suffering from the symptoms of schizophrenia, patients who have never been tried on lithium. Never. I know there are others like Ned — Jane who is an honor student, Bill who is a star baseball player, Nancy who likes to dance, Tom, Frank and Barbara. All of them are patients of mine who are lithium responders with renewed hope. They are now able to work, to attend school, to live independently, and to pursue their dreams.

But there are still others who NEVER HAVE BEEN TRIED ON LITHIUM — 100,000, 200,000, 300,000 — many who would respond, but HAVE NOT YET BEEN TRIED ON LITHIUM.

Why not?

A very important question. I have asked it myself, but I have not discovered any reasonable answer. When I consulted at a community mental health center, I put one hundred patients who were diagnosed as suffering from schizophrenia on lithium. Fifty-five patients tolerated the medication and remained on it; thirty-five of these patients showed good improvements. Many of them went to work and were able to live independently.

Despite published scientific research studies that demonstrate these outcomes, there is still a reluctance to use lithium. Maybe this reluctance stems from fearfulness about lithium, yet, in fact, there are few side effects, few toxic effects. It is safe and dependable. Maybe there is a hesitancy to use lithium because of the periodic laboratory tests that are required to ensure the patient is receiving a therapeutic dosage. Maybe the hesitancy is because psychiatrists think they can separate lithium responders from non-responders by evaluating presenting symptoms. From my professional experience, I have learned this cannot be done.

What I most want to stress is that many patients who have been diagnosed as suffering from the symptoms of schizophrenia would respond to lithium if only they were tried on it. Some of these patients are our family members, our sons and daughters, our brothers and sisters. They may respond as Ned did. His life has been transformed, revolutionized by a trial of lithium. That is all it took, just a trial, but it worked. Who knows, maybe your family member would also respond. Insist that your loved one be given a trial on lithium.

There is hope — yes, hope not only in lithium but in other medications. There is hope for those who suffer from chronic illness. There is a way out of the sadness that grips families, dashes dreams, and destroys lives. Yes, hope. And there will be more hope as time goes on; new medications will be added to the ones we already have. With these discoveries we will have developed new ways of treating patients who suffer from these illnesses.

Yes, there is hope.

2

Etiology: How do we get these illnesses?

How does a person get schizophrenia? This very simple question has been a difficult one to answer. Early theories pointed to the patient's mother as the cause of the patient's illness. There was even a term "schizophrenogenic mother" to describe the maternal qualities that were believed to cause schizophrenia. Then there were psychiatrists who proposed that families caused schizophrenia. According to these theorists, parents who did not communicate very well with their children and put their children in impossible situations contributed to the children's diseases. Impossible situations were those in which the children reacted one way and were made to feel that they had made a wrong choice; however, if they reacted in another way, their choice was considered wrong also. This was called the double bind theory. Children were thought to have reacted to these situations by becoming psychotic. This theory was popular for quite a while.

Research has in fact proven that certain families produce children who have the symptoms of schizophrenia. Is this correlation due to environmental factors or genes?

If you look at the genetic information that is available from scientific studies, you find that the incidence of schizophrenia is about 1 percent of the population of the United States — for that matter 1 percent of the population of the world. So just by being born, you have one chance in one hundred of getting the illness. If your mother or father suffered from schizophrenia, you have a 10 percent chance of getting the illness. If both your parents suffered from schizophrenia, then your chances jump to 40 percent. If you have a brother or sister who has the illness, you also have a 10 percent chance of getting it. Now if you have an identical twin who suffers from schizophrenia, you have a 50 percent chance of getting this illness. The incidence, however, is only 15 percent in non-identical twins.

So what does this data tell us? The closer a relative is genetically to a person with schizophrenia, the greater the probability that the relative will also get this illness.

Twin studies also give us insight into the problem of etiology. We can study twins who live in the same environment and share the same — or almost the same — genetic structure, identical twins, and compare them with twins who live in the same environment and do not share the same genetic make-up, non-identical twins.

Schizophrenia — Genetic Factors

1% Population has Schizophrenia
10% If Mother or Father has Schizophrenia
10% If Brother or Sister has Schizophrenia
40% If both Mother and Father have Schizophrenia
50% If Monozygotic (Identical) Twin has Schizophrenia
15% If Dizygotic (Non-identical) Twin has Schizophrenia

Figure 2.1

If schizophrenia is caused by environmental influences and not genetic influences, then twins brought up in the same families would have almost the same environmental influences. Genes would not play a part in this illness. One would expect that if one twin developed the symptoms of schizophrenia, the other one would develop symptoms also, regardless of the genetic make-up of the twins. That has not been the case. In the same environment, the concordance rate is 15 percent for the non-identical twin and 50 percent for the identical one. Even if the twins are separated at birth, as may occur in adoption, and one twin suffers from the symptoms of schizophrenia, the concordance rate is still around 15 percent in the non-identical twins and 50 percent in the identical twins. The environments are different, but the genetic make-up is the same — this finding points to a strong genetic factor in this illness.

The question that is always asked at this point is, "Why isn't the concordance rate in the identical twins one hundred percent?" The explanation is in the genetic structure of identical twins. In fact, identical twins are not completely identical in genetic structure. When genetic structure folds or bends, it alters the genetic make-up somewhat. This variation allows for the 50 percent concordance rate; it can be explained by folding alone.

Psychiatry is becoming increasingly biological. Genes play important roles in the etiology of the illnesses psychiatrists treat. This fact means that brain chemistry will play an even more important role in psychiatry than it does now. Laboratory studies will give us better diagnostic skills so that patients will not be misdiagnosed. We will be able to diagnose patients by testing urine and blood samples for different compounds. At the present time, my colleagues and I are looking at compounds found in the urine specimens of our patients for clues that will be beneficial in accurate diagnoses. Most importantly, patients will benefit from increasingly reliable biological tests that will promote accurate diagnosis and apporopriate treatment.

3

Diagnosing: How can we do this accurately?

For the patient and family, the problems associated with chronic illness can be long term. Nevertheless, these illnesses and their problems can be addressed in a more timely, efficient way when the diagnosis is accurate.

Ned's problem started seven years ago. Finding the solution did not need to be a seven-year ordeal for Ned and his family, but Ned was misdiagnosed — yes, misdiagnosed. Unfortunately, misdiagnosis is not all that uncommon.

When I taught at the University of Louisville, I consulted for five years at the community mental health center. There I re-evaluated every patient I saw; approximately 50 percent were misdiagnosed. They were diagnosed as suffering from the symptoms of schizophrenia, but in fact they were misdiagnosed. They had the symptoms of schizoaffective disorder or bipolar disorder, but not the symptoms of patients suffering from schizophrenia.

Ned was diagnosed when he was in the acute psychotic state when all these illnesses have similar symptoms. In this state an accurate diagnosis cannot be reached. The problem is that psychiatrists diagnose patients in this state, and the diagnosis usually lasts. Rarely is the diagnosis changed during the next few days when the patient comes out of the acute state.

It is important to recognize that the patient is acutely psychotic. The problem arises when psychiatrists try to differentiate schizophrenia from bipolar disorder. One just cannot do that effectively during the acute state. Unfortunately, Ned was diagnosed as a patient suffering from the symptoms of schizophrenia during his first psychotic episode. When I saw him seven years later, he was still diagnosed that way. No one bothered to rethink his diagnosis, and, as a result, his medication remained the same: antipsychotics such as Thorazine, Stelazine, Haldol. He was never tried on lithium. Alternatives were not considered. Because of this failure to reassess his diagnosis, Ned lost seven valuable years.

Making an initial diagnosis, that is, a diagnosis when the patient is first evaluated, is important. But when the patient is in an acutely psychotic state, the initial diagnosis should be an acute psychotic state; further delineation is just not possible with any degree of accuracy. Further diagnostic possibilities need to be considered and investigated. Is the problem due to drugs? An infection? Temporal lobe epilepsy? A brain tumor? All these considerations are somewhat easy to eliminate through the completion of specific diagnostic procedures, such as lab tests, electroencephalograms, CT scans, and other tests depending on the patient's symptoms.

So then, how should a psychiatrist go about making a diagnosis? It is clear that when the patient is acutely psychotic, the psychiatrist cannot make an accurate diagnosis.

Ned was initially evaluated in the emergency room of a downtown city hospital. At first he was examined by an emergency room physician; a physical exam was carried out and a brief history was obtained from his parents. I suspect that some lab studies were also ordered. Ned's psychotic state was quite apparent to the emergency room physician who notified the psychiatrist on call. He then came and evaluated Ned.

At that time Ned appeared acutely psychotic: he was actively hallucinating; he was paranoid; his affect was blunted and flat. In addition he had a history of not sleeping. The psychiatrist on call diagnosed Ned as suffering from the symptoms of paranoid schizophrenia. Now, to be fair, Ned had all the signs and symptoms that could lead to that diagnosis, but many patients suffering from bipolar illness also exhibit these signs and symptoms when they become acutely psychotic. They hallucinate; they can be delusional and paranoid, and they do not sleep well. These many similarities are the reason why diagnosing patients in this state is so difficult. The symptoms appear to be those of a patient suffering from schizophrenia, but the illness may not be schizophrenia.

Ned's diagnosis was not changed — not after he came out of the acute psychotic state, not after he left the hospital, not after he was seen as an outpatient or admitted again to the hospital, not even when he was evaluated by other psychiatrists. The diagnosis remained the same. He was even re-evaluated at the medical school near his home town. He was repeatedly diagnosed as suffering from the symptoms of schizophrenia. No one picked up on the fact that maybe Ned was suffering from something else. What is shocking to me as a psychiatrist is that a devastating diagnosis, such as schizophrenia, is rarely questioned once it is on a hospital chart. Now, I am not saying that schizophrenia does not exist. I wish it did not, but it does. What I do want to convey is that psychiatrists make this diagnosis too soon, too often. And once they have made the diagnosis, they are very reluctant to re-evaluate the patient and change the diagnosis. Earlier in my career, I would pride myself into thinking that I could diagnose schizophrenia accurately when a patient was acutely psychotic in the emergency room. I have since learned that diagnosing in the acute state cannot be done. Yet I still see patients repeatedly misdiagnosed with schizophrenia.

The main diagnostic dilemma is in differentiating schizophrenia from bipolar disorder. There was a time in the 1950s and '60s when psychiatrists were very broad in the diagnosing of schizophrenia and very narrow in the diagnosing of bipolar disorder. Every illness that had even the slightest symptom of schizophrenia was labeled schizophrenia, no matter how many symptoms of bipolar disorder were present. Then we discovered that psychiatrists in England were diagnosing schizophrenia much less frequently than psychiatrists in the United States, and we too began re-evaluating the problem of diagnosis.

Schizophrenia	Bipolar Disorder

Figure 3.1

Further review indicated that some patients who were suffering from schizophrenia did better than others. This differentiation created two groups of patients: those identified with a good prognosis and those identified with a poor prognosis. More patients were now included in the bipolar group, rather than in the schizophrenia classification. Along with presenting symptoms, family history and natural history of the illness were found to be important in making the diagnosis.

Schizophrenia		Bipolar Disorder
Poor Prognosis	Good Prognosis	

Figure 3.2

As time went on, studies indicated that the patients who were in the good prognosis category in many ways resembled patients who were suffering from bipolar disorder. Patients in this good prognosis category had mood swings; they became excited, had grandiose delusions, and had problems sleeping. They also hallucinated and were often paranoid. These patients were hard to classify. They were somewhere between schizophrenia and bipolar disorder; thus, a new category, schizoaffective illness, was formed. This new diagnostic category helped us look closer at the diagnostic dilemmas of schizophrenia. A closer look makes sense; we do not want to make this diagnosis any more often than it is clearly indicated.

Schizophrenia	Schizoaffective	Bipolar Disorder

Figure 3.3

With all the dilemmas and ambiguity involved in diagnosis, the inevitable question arises: Why is making a diagnosis so important? There are many reasons why, ranging from treatment issues to expected patient outcomes. One of the most important reasons, however, is that a diagnosis governs what kinds of medication will be tried. If a patient is diagnosed as suffering from bipolar disorder, then lithium will be tried. If, on the other hand, the patient is suffering from the symptoms of schizophrenia, then antipsychotic medications, such as Haldol and Thorazine, are used — not lithium.

Furthermore, as discussed, another important issue in diagnosis is the implication arising from it. Erasing the diagnosis from charts and patient records creates problems; even more difficult is erasing this diagnosis from the minds of the patients and families. As much as we hope society has progressed, certain diagnoses still carry stigmas and consequences that can be very detrimental to patients. In view of these issues, the importance of accurate diagnosis becomes clear.

When making a diagnosis, I look at the following three aspects of the patient: presenting symptoms, natural history of the illness and family history. Each of these is important in determining the diagnosis.

---

3 Aspects of Diagnosis

1. Presenting Symptoms

2. Natural History of the Illness

3. Family History

Figure 3.4

Presenting symptoms are my first consideration. Presenting symptoms refer to the patient's thought processes, affect, behavior and perception. Sometimes presenting symptoms are clearly apparent through the patient's actions and statements.

Presenting Symptoms

Thinking

Mood, Affect

Behavior

Perception

Figure 3.5

At other times additional questioning may be necessary. If a family member is present, the task is easier for the psychiatrist and less stressful for the patient. Family members can usually fill in some details about the patient's symptoms.

When a patient is suffering from a thought disorder, such as schizophrenia, the patient's thought process is affected. I usually look at this symptom first. The individual's thoughts may reflect delusions, or false beliefs a person has. With delusional thinking, no amount of reasoning will dissuade the person from believing the thoughts are true. In Ned's case, he was convinced his roommate, teachers, and friends were all against him.

Delusions can be present in the patient's thinking in a variety of ways. Some delusions are religious delusions in which patients may believe God is speaking directly to them or calling them to a special place. Somatic delusions are delusions that relate to the body, such as beliefs that one has a computer inside him that tells him what to do. Somatic delusions can also reflect fears in which patients can believe insects or outside forces have entered the body and are eating their intestines. Often I hear patients refer to these outside forces as powers that are controlling their lives. They believe these forces put thoughts in their minds and can tell them whom to trust and what to do. These voices can be dangerous if they tell a patient to kill himself or someone else.

Sometimes my patients think their thoughts will be broadcast or written on the walls of buildings so that everyone can see what they are thinking. As part of their delusions, patients may invent their own language and develop words, neologisms, that make sense to them but are not related to reality.

Patients experiencing thought disorders often speak in very concrete terms. If I ask them what the saying, "Don't cry over spilled milk," means to them, these patients may answer, "You don't cry over spilled milk; you just mop it up."

When evaluating the patient's thought process, I am also careful to look for symptoms of mania, such as grandiose thinking, pressured speech, irritability, anger, hyperactivity, decreased sleep, and decreased need for sleep. Signs of depression I look for include decreased energy levels, difficulty sleeping, and loss of appetite. I want to be sure I am not overlooking any signs of bipolar or affective disorders.

Thinking is not the only area I examine, but it is the one in which I find major distortions. Awareness of these distortions is a vital step in reaching a diagnosis.

I also look at the mood or affect of my patients — in everyday terms this means their emotions. Often there is no emotion conveyed at all. Their affect is flat or blunted; this manifestation is most apparent in their face, which is expressionless as if there is no emotional contact. Interacting with them is almost like talking to a stone; there is just no response. I know there is a person behind this flat affect, but the patient expresses no emotional contact. Flat affect is one clue to what's going on, since affect is a very authentic indicator of the patient's mental state. A flat affect is hard, if not impossible, to manufacture; thus, it is a presenting symptom that the psychiatrist must consider when making a diagnosis.

Patients may also present with an excited or agitated affect. They may be so manic or hyper in behavior and expression that they cannot control themselves and may need staff assistance to regain self-control. This can be an emergency situation that requires immediate attention to ensure the patient's safety.

Emotions can also fluctuate, and the patients will go from flat to excited, up and down. Likewise, their moods may be incongruent to the context; thus, they may laugh when listening to something sad, or cry when the appropriate response should be laughter.

A third aspect of presenting symptoms that I observe is behavior. When observing affect, I am looking primarily at how the patient conveys emotion; with behavior, I am considering what the patient is actually doing and in what manner. Is he moving fast, so-called climbing the walls? Is he withdrawn, showing little or no interest in doing anything? Is he catatonic, completely unable to talk, communicate or make any gesture without direction and assistance from someone else?

Some patients' behavior may be bizarre with facial grimacing and body posturing. They stand out in a crowd, yet they are very isolated with few friends. They often do not function well. In Ned's case, he had not been able to work or go to school for seven years. He had few friends, if any, and did not go out much. This lifestyle is not reflective of a twenty-seven year old man.

The fourth aspect of presenting symptoms is perception. Perception refers to how the patient experiences sensory material. Most of us validate the world through our senses of sight, hearing, touch, taste, and smell. In essence we perceive the world through our senses. When perception is altered, such as occurs in these illnesses, an individual experiences sensory information that is not based on the external world. Patients are said to hallucinate because they see, hear, feel, taste, or smell things that are not present in reality.

Ned saw images and heard voices that were not real except to him. This is a common finding among patients, but not one exclusively found in patients suffering from schizophrenia. At one time psychiatrists and other mental health professionals believed hallucinations always indicated schizophrenia. This belief is not true — that belief was wrong then and it is wrong now. There are no symptoms exclusively diagnostic of schizophrenia. None. In studies of bipolar patients diagnosed according to strict research and diagnostic criteria, hallucinations were often present. We now recognize that patients who suffer from bipolar disorder do hallucinate.

What is markedly different between bipolar disorder and schizophrenia is the natural history of the illness in the patient's life. If you look at the natural history of an illness — when it starts, what happens after its onset, what level of functioning the patient maintains or progresses to — this history offers clues to diagnosis. The natural histories of schizophrenia and bipolar disorder are different. For instance, the onset of schizophrenia is earlier in life, usually during the adolescent or young adult years; bipolar disorder usually appears in a person's early thirties.

After observing and getting a history of the presenting symptoms, I review the natural history of the illness in the patient's life. Often this history provides information which will differentiate a diagnosis of schizophrenia from a diagnosis of bipolar disorder. Several key issues are pertinent when evaluating the history of the illness: the patient's age at the time of first symptoms, the severity of symptoms, the length of episodes when symptoms were most severe and the level of functioning that the patient can maintain when not suffering severe symptoms.

Figure 3.6 depicts a graph of the natural history of schizophrenia. Around age twenty a patient usually suffers from an

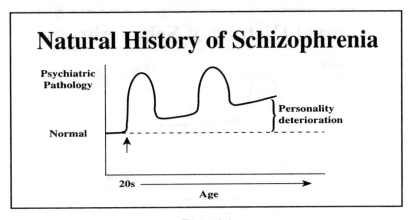

Figure 3.6

acute psychotic episode. This episode means the patient will need hospitalization and medication. When the patient is discharged from the hospital, he obviously cannot live as he did before hospitalization. Patients often cannot go back to school, cannot hold down a job or live independently. The negative symptoms of schizophrenia continue: blunted affect, withdrawal, isolation, lethargy and absence of motivation. These negative symptoms are called personality deterioration. Patients just do not return to their pre-illness state of functioning. There is a wide range of individual differences in patients who suffer from schizophrenia. Some patients function better than others, but the great majority show the signs of schizophrenia after they are discharged from the hospital and out of the acute phase of the illness.

Some patients, around 25 percent, who show the presenting symptoms of an acute psychotic episode do respond to medications and do not have any more episodes. They do not have the residual signs of schizophrenia either. They resume normal lives. This pattern is exemplified in the graph depicted in Figure 3.7.

A different pattern is shown in Figure 3.8. Patients with this form of schizophrenia show many negative symptoms. They exhibit personality deterioration without acute psychotic episodes. The onset again is around age twenty, but I have seen patients with onset as young as sixteen. Patients slowly move into a more vegetative state over time. They also lose their ability to work, to attend school, or to live independently.

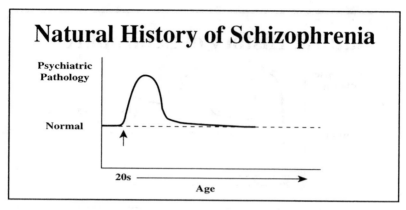

Figure 3.7

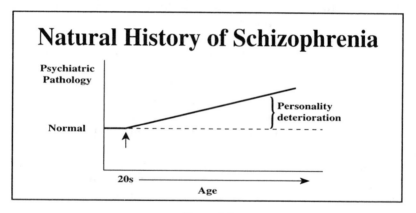

Figure 3.8

Patients who suffer from the symptoms of bipolar disorder are different from those who suffer from the symptoms of schizophrenia. The onset of the illness is later in life, usually around age thirty. Patients usually become psychotic while in the manic phase of the illness. They can become delusional and paranoid, and they can hallucinate. Between episodes of the illness, however, patients with bipolar disorder tend to go back to whatever normal living was for them. They do not suffer from personality deterioration, withdrawal, and inability to work or go to school. They do not have the blunted affect of patients suffering from the symptoms of schizophrenia, and often patients with bipolar disorder can live

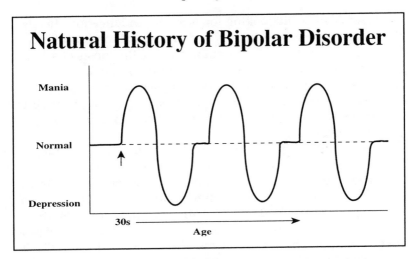

Figure 3.9

independently between episodes of their illness. Figure 3.9 reveals a graph of the natural history of bipolar disorder.

By picturing the natural history of an illness on a graph, patterns become clear. These patterns are valuable in determining the diagnosis. Often the patient's family members are of utmost importance in providing information on the history of the illness in the patient's life.

Understanding the history of the illness in the patient's life is crucial. Along with presenting symptoms, the history of the illness provides information that is relevant to reaching a diagnosis.

The third component of a diagnostic evaluation is family history. We know that schizophrenia and bipolar disorder run in families. There is a general rule of thumb that families that produce children who suffer from schizophrenia are different genetically from families that produce children who suffer from bipolar disorder. I try to find out if there are family members who suffer from mental illness. Sometimes this relative is an aunt or uncle, or a grandmother who died in the state hospital. I try to find a clue to the diagnosis of these family members. I look for depression, alcoholism, or bipolar disorder — these point to a history of affective or mood disorders in the family. A positive history of schizophrenia in family members points to a diagnosis of schizophrenia.

What I am really looking for is some evidence for affective disorders in the family history. I do not want to miss affective disorders, because maybe, just maybe, the diagnosis of schizophrenia is not the correct diagnosis. I am always looking for a good reason to change the diagnosis of schizophrenia to something else. Often changing the diagnosis is appropriate, and this opens the door to a different treatment approach that frequently proves to be very effective.

Presenting symptoms, the patient's life history after the first psychotic episode, and family history — all these factors need to be evaluated before an accurate diagnosis can be achieved.

In Ned's case, he had a maternal aunt who suffered from depression. He also had an uncle and grandfather who suffered from alcoholism. These facts revealed that Ned's family had produced children who suffered from affective disorders. Ned's illness probably fell in that category also. Ned's history revealed that he had a strong probability of having schizoaffective illness or bipolar illness. These factors supported a trial on lithium.

Clues indicating Ned's diagnosis were present throughout his treatment. They were visible in the presenting symptoms, the affect and the behavior. They were also there in the family history. Why these clues were missed, I do not know. They were there, however, and missing this crucial evidence cost Ned years of productive life. Moreover, it cost both Ned and his parents years of emotional suffering.

With accurate diagnosis and treatment, Ned can now experience a more productive life, but the seven years cannot be replaced. I wish I could say that misdiagnosis and ineffective treatment are uncommon, but the truth is both happen all too often. In community mental health centers, state hospitals, acute inner city psychiatric units under the direction of medical school's psychiatric departments, private psychiatric hospitals — in virtually all treatment settings — inaccurate diagnosis and inadequate treatment are more common than we suspect.

These inaccuracies should not be so prevalent. One day, hopefully, all we will need is a blood sample or urine specimen from the patient, and we will be able to come to an accurate diagnosis through a laboratory test. Until that day, though, the families of patients need to understand the importance of presenting symptoms, natural history of the patient's illness, and family history. By understanding these factors, family members can give valuable information about their loved one's illness to the psychiatrist.

As family members, you can do more. You can participate in the selection of the treatment the patient receives. You can insist that lithium be tried. I recommend that you find a psychiatrist who will try lithium. Seek information, ask questions, and read. Make sure everything is being done without missing any clues.

4

Treatment: What options are there?

Schizophrenia is a brain disease. It has to do with abnormal brain chemistry. To treat this illness, the brain chemistry must be changed. For a long time we have had medications, called antipsychotics, that would change brain chemistry, but these medications have been greatly limited.

The history of these antipsychotic medications dates back to the 1950s when Thorazine (generic name, chlorpromazine hydrochloride) was discovered. Originally Thorazine was used as a drying agent for patients undergoing surgery. It dried up secretions in the nose, mouth and lungs. In 1952 it was tried as a medication for schizophrenia. Researchers then discovered that it calmed psychotic patients and altered their delusions and hallucinations. Further observations showed that Thorazine was useful in bringing patients out of an acutely psychotic state. Up until that time, the only medications available were sedating medications that did not alter the psychotic state. Thorazine was a major breakthrough.

One of the limitations involved with antipsychotics, such as Thorazine, is their potential to cause side effects. All medications have the potential to cause side effects, even though not all patients experience side effects.

The potential side effects of Thorazine range from bothersome to dangerous. Sedation is a side effect that is bothersome. Patients often feel tired, lethargic, and "drugged out" after taking Thorazine. Patients may also complain of dry mouth and constipation. At times patients suffer from movement disorders. They may experience joint stiffness, tremors in the hands, or movements in the arms, neck, face. They can also feel light-headed and dizzy when they stand or move suddenly. Lightheadedness is due to a decrease in blood pressure which can be a side effect of Thorazine. Though these side effects are bothersome, they are generally not dangerous and can be monitored by the patient's physician and family.

Antipsychotic Medication Side Effects

1. **Sedation**

2. **Autonomic Nervous System**
   a. Lightheadedness
   b. Dry Mouth, Nasal Congestion
   c. Blurred Vision
   d. Constipation

3. **Endocrine System**
   a. Increased Prolactin Level
      1. Breast Enlargement
      2. Impotence in Males
      3. Amenorrhea
   b. Weight Gain

4. **Skin**
   a. Pigmentation in Areas Exposed to Sunlight
   b. Photosensitivity

5. **Neurological Side Effects**
   a. Dystonia — Spasm — Tongue, Jaw and Neck
   b. Muscle Stiffness
   c. Rigidity of Joints
   d. Stooped Posture
   e. Drooling
   f. Akinesia — Reduction in Voluntary Movements
   g. Akathisia — Inner Restlessness
   h. Tardive Dyskinesia

Figure 4.1

Antipsychotic medications are not very effective in eliminating the negative symptoms of schizophrenia. The negative symptoms to which I am referring include withdrawal, blunted affect, inability to work or go to school, and the decline in ability to function independently, which patients suffering from schizophrenia often experience.

Despite their limitations, these medications are effective in several very significant ways. They are effective in getting patients out of an acute psychotic state, and they are effective in reducing the incidence of hospital readmissions.

In the treatment of schizophrenia, I divide the use of these medications into two phases: the acute phase of treatment and the post-acute phase of treatment. This division serves to distinguish the maximum benefit these medications can offer in the treatment process.

Acute Phase of Treatment

The acute phase of treatment is the phase which focuses on getting the patient out of an acute psychotic break. During an acute psychotic break, a patient may hallucinate, become paranoid, combative, suicidal. The patient is very vulnerable, and I consider this phase a medical emergency. The patient needs to be hospitalized and started on medication.

For patients in an acute psychotic state, the world can be a terrifying place, a place where they can trust no one and a place where everything is beyond their control or understanding. When Bill showed up in our emergency room, he was in an acute psychotic state. It was a bitter cold January morning. He walked up to the information desk and asked, "What time does the zest begin?"

When the nurse told him that she did not hear him, and to repeat the question, Bill said, "The ship has come and I'm going nowhere. If you tell God, I'll die." Then Bill began pacing back and forth, mumbling to himself. The staff was able to bring Bill to a triage room where we proceeded with a psychiatric evaluation. As I evaluated him, I found that he was hallucinating, confused, and agitated. He had a history of not sleeping and had been afraid to eat because he believed his stomach was in hell. Bill was acutely psychotic. He needed to be hospitalized and started on medication. I considered his case a medical emergency. He was vulnerable, and with his paranoid thoughts, he could become combative or suicidal.

When patients are in an acute phase, they need a thorough physical exam, including standard laboratory tests: a CBC, SMA 20, urinalysis. Usually these tests come back in the normal range. Bill's tests all came back within the normal range, and his physical exam was also within normal limits. While he was still in the emergency room, I ordered 200 milligrams of Thorazine for him and arranged for his admission to the hospital's psychiatric unit.

While the patient is in the emergency room or as soon as he is admitted to the hospital's psychiatric unit, I order 200 milligrams of Thorazine to be given immediately. Within a short time, this medication will usually have a calming effect on the patient. This dose is repeated at two hour intervals, so that by the end of four hours, the patient has received a total of 600 milligrams of Thorazine. Often patients go to sleep during this time. When they wake up, they are usually better; their hallucinations are not as prominent, and they are not as paranoid. Overall, their state of agitation and excitement has been toned down.

This regimen of medication dosage and frequency is called rapid neuroleptization. It means that patients are given high doses of medication over a short period of time in an effort to get them out of the acute psychotic state rapidly. Certainly this method of treatment is effective in treating the patient in the acute psychotic state of the illness. I believe there is some value to rapid neuroleptization. Not everyone agrees. There is reliable evidence that lower doses of medication are just as effective as rapid neuroleptization, at least in the long run. We used this method in the seventies and early eighties, and it was effective for us.

For the next two to three days, a patient needs 300 to 400 milligrams of Thorazine every six hours around the clock. After two to three days of these high doses, a patient usually comes out of his acute psychotic break. The advantage of Thorazine is its sedating effects. Sedation is usually helpful to patients in the acute psychotic state. There are side effects, such as decreases in blood pressure, but these are usually small decreases in the pressure; they do not last long, and are easy to control.

In my experience, patients improve rapidly on this medication regimen. I studied 100 consecutive patients who were admitted to our unit and treated this way. When they came into the hospital, they were acutely psychotic. The average length of stay was sixteen days. These patients were turned around rapidly using this method of treatment. There is no good scientific evidence that longer hospital stays are of more therapeutic value than shorter hospital stays. As a matter of fact, the opposite may be true. Often family members feel that a longer hospital stay is of more value, that patients will somehow find out what is behind their illness and will come out of the hospital much better or even cured. That supposition just is not true, although I wish it were.

Bill's case is an example of what we experienced in treating patients on our psychiatric unit. During the first four hours he was in the hospital, he received a total of 600 milligrams of Thorazine. He responded by going to sleep. In the morning he was given an additional 400 milligrams of Thorazine. This dosage was repeated three more times that day. Bill received 1600 milligrams of Thorazine for the next three days. He was sleeping and eating better; he was not as delusional; his hallucinations were not as prevalent. He had calmed down and was coming out of the acute phase of the illness.

Post-Acute Phase of Treatment

The goal of the post-acute phase of treatment is different from that of the acute phase. In the acute phase, the goal of treatment is to treat the patient in an acute psychotic episode— in essence to get the patient over this acute state. The goal of the post-acute phase is to stabilize the patient on the least amount of medication necessary for him to be discharged from the hospital and resume his highest level of functioning. In addition, this phase focuses on maintaining this level of functioning so that the patient does not need to be rehospitalized. This phase is a process that involves a lot of work, and it is a process that involves psychiatrists, nurses, social workers, the patient, and often the family members.

The conventional antipsychotics that we use, e.g., Haldol, Thorazine, Stelazine, Navane, Prolixin, etc., are effective in getting patients out of the acute phase of their illness. These medications also help prevent relapse and rehospitalization, but they are not very effective in helping patients resume whatever normal functioning and living was for them prior to their illness. On these medications alone, many patients cannot work, go to school, or live independently. Often these patients just vegetate. Many live with their biological families or in halfway houses. More often than we admit, many of these patients have no place to live and end up in the streets or in jail.

Many issues are involved in this problem of patients' outpatient placement and residence. It is a problem with no quick-fixes or simple solutions, but it is a problem that we need to address with compassion and knowledge. Central to any and all solutions is the patient's ongoing need for medication. The right medication at the right dose will help maximize the patient's opportunities for independent functioning. Determining which medication and dosage is needed is part of medication management in this post-acute phase of treatment.

When patients like Bill recover from the acute psychotic state, their dose of Thorazine can be cut back rapidly. In the acute phase of the illness, patients can end up on 1600 to 2000, even 2400, milligrams of Thorazine a day. When patients come out of this phase of the illness, their dose of Thorazine can be reduced rapidly over a period of days until the patient is on 400 milligrams of Thorazine a day. Then I add lithium 300 milligrams twice a day. If at any time during this dosage reduction, the psychotic symptoms recur, then the Thorazine dose is increased and the lithium is discontinued. Usually patients move through these medication changes with no difficulties.

Bill's Thorazine was decreased from 1600 milligrams a day to 1200 milligrams by the fifth day he was on the psychiatric unit. On day six, the dose was cut to 800 milligrams; on day seven, the dose was further reduced to 400 milligrams taken at night before Bill went to bed. The next morning, Bill was given 300 milligrams of lithium. The dose was repeated at bedtime. Bill also was given 400 milligrams of Thorazine at bedtime. He continued on 400 milligrams of Thorazine and 300 milligrams of lithium twice a day for the next four days. Then a lithium blood level was drawn to determine if this dosage was bringing the medication to a therapeutic level for Bill. The blood test showed the medication was in the therapeutic range. Bill continued to improve and was discharged from the hospital on day twelve on Thorazine and lithium.

When the dose of Thorazine is reduced to the lowest dose at which the patient can be maintained, lithium is added. During the post-acute phase, one of my primary goals is determining if the patient is a lithium responder. Dr. John Cade started using lithium in Australia in 1948. He tried it on patients suffering from bipolar illness and schizophrenia. The bipolar patients did very well, and lithium has been used in their treatment ever since. He also had some favorable results in patients suffering from the symptoms of schizophrenia, but the change in them was not as dramatic.

Lithium is my favorite medication for stabilizing patients after an acute psychotic break. Because lithium can be extremely effective, I try all my patients on it for at least six months. If patients respond to lithium, they have a good chance of working, going to school, living independently. On the regimen of Thorazine and lithium, Bill was able to return to work. His symptoms were gone; he was motivated; he looked much better.

There are other medications that have the same effect that lithium does. Tegretol (generic name, carbamazepine) and Depakote (valproate) were originally used to treat seizure disorders. Their use in treatment for these disorders continues, but we have also found that these medications are useful in stabilizing patients after an acute psychotic episode. If I don't get the results I want with lithium, that is, if the patient does not experience an increased ability to function independently, then I add Depakote. I may also add Tegretol. In combination with lithium, these medications give us options. Patients respond to them; we need to try patients on these medications.

Let me tell you about Jeff and how the combination of medications was beneficial to him. Jeff came into the emergency room in an acute psychotic state. He was hallucinating, delusional, and excited. He had not slept much the prior three or four nights. He had some grandiose thinking and racing thoughts. Furthermore, he had a positive family history for affective disorder. After coming out of the acute psychotic state, Jeff was stabilized on lithium.

In three weeks, after he was discharged from the hospital, he was off his antipsychotic medications. He did quite well for four weeks. Then he again became delusional, hallucinated, and could not sleep. The acute psychotic symptoms were returning. This time he was stabilized on Thorazine out of the hospital and did not require readmission. After stabilization he was restarted on lithium. This time Depakote was added to the lithium. He received 250 milligrams four times a day. Again the Thorazine dose was reduced and finally discontinued. Jeff did well. The lithium and Depakote were effective in controlling his psychotic symptoms. He did not need to be on antipsychotic medications.

Six months later I tried to get Jeff off lithium to see if Depakote would be effective by itself in keeping the psychotic symptoms from breaking through. This discontinuance did not work. In four weeks Jeff experienced a recurrence of his symptoms. I had to restart the lithium. This combination worked. Jeff was maintained quite well on the combination of medicines; while on one or the other alone, he was not. Jeff is one of many patients who benefit from the combination of medications.

New Medications

In addition to the conventional antipsychotics, lithium, Tegretol and Depakote, there are other medications which are effective in treatment. Clozaril (generic name, clozapine) is a medication that has been available for use in treatment since the 1970s. As with other medications, Clozaril has side effects, the major one being suppression of bone marrow. This is a serious side effect that can be fatal, and in the late 1970s Clozaril's use was discontinued because of deaths due to bone marrow suppression. Dr. Herbert Meltzer of Case Western Reserve Medical School has opened the door for us to use this medication again. Its use has resumed, and Clozaril is regarded as safe when the patient's white blood cell count is monitored carefully. Monitoring can be done by weekly laboratory tests.

When used with this monitoring, Clozaril is a magnificent medication. The results have been overwhelming. Patients get better. Not only do they lose their delusions and hallucinations, but they also lose many of the so-called negative symptoms. Patients are not as withdrawn or isolated. They tend to socialize and go out more. Many are able to hold down jobs. Some go back to school. Often they can live more independently. This independence is extremely good news. When there has been little or no response to lithium, Tegretol, or Depakote, a trial on

Clozaril is in order. With Clozaril we have an antipsychotic medication that not only treats the acute psychotic episode and keeps patients out of the hospital, but also adds to the quality of their lives by reducing negative symptoms. More patients need to be tried on this medication; more patients need to be offered the chance to experience an improved quality of life.

Risperdal (generic name, risperidone) is another antipsychotic medication that offers new opportunities to enhance a patient's quality of life. This medication is now on the market and results of trial studies are promising. In one study that involved 135 chronic patients, Risperdal was tested against Haldol and a placebo under double-blind conditions, that is, neither the doctors nor the patients knew who was on the medication. Risperdal at a dose of 6 milligrams was superior to placebo and Haldol in the alleviation of both the positive symptoms and negative symptoms. Positive symptoms include the delusions, hallucinations, excitement, sleep disturbance, and reality distortion that patients experience; negative symptoms include the withdrawal, blunted affect, and personality deterioration seen in patients with schizophrenia. The effect of Risperdal was very similar to the effect of Clozaril on a similar group of chronic, refractory patients. Risperdal was superior to Haldol in the alleviation of negative symptoms. Furthermore, Risperdal does not suppress bone marrow like Clozaril can, so weekly blood tests are not necessary. In addition, with Risperdal, patients experience fewer Parkinsonian symptoms and a decrease in dyskinetic movements as compared to patients on Haldol. These are troubling side effects of Haldol and some of the other conventional antipsychotic medications.

Risperdal appears to have a therapeutic profile similar to medications classified as atypical antipsychotic medications like Clozaril. This effect was seen on both positive and negative symptoms. These results are favorable not only in terms of this study but also in the context of the future. The availability of new medications which can offer greater treatment options for patients is important. We need to provide treatment that enriches patients' quality of life and enables them to reach their highest level of functioning.

5
A Treatment Model

As early as childhood, most of us have had some experience with hospitals. We may have many different feelings about these settings, but at least we have some frame of reference and experience that helps us understand the purpose and value of hospitals.

Your understanding of psychiatric hospitals and treatment may have been influenced by many different factors. You may have misconceptions about treatment settings based on what you have seen on television, at the movies, or in magazines and books. You may wonder what really happens in a psychiatric treatment unit.

After quite a few years as a psychiatrist associated with a variety of treatment settings, I can say that psychiatric care may vary greatly from one treatment setting to another. State and national licensing agencies set standards of care, but the actual treatment approach may vary significantly from one setting to another.

From 1975 to 1986, I was director of Psychiatric Services at Louisville General Hospital. Though the actual building was outdated, the treatment rendered patients was of the highest professional quality. To this day, I still consider that treatment program a model approach and one with which I feel fortunate to have been associated. For many years I have asked myself what set this program above the others. Furthermore, I have examined what aspects of this program could be important to you in evaluating treatment settings for your family member.

One of the most crucial issues to consider is the treatment team. At the University of Louisville the treatment team was comprised of highly trained nurses, social workers, art and occupational therapists, and psychiatric residents. In addition this team included medical students, chaplain and nursing students.

The head nurse set the tone of the unit; she had excellent diagnostic insight and was highly skilled in psychopharmacology. Frequently she picked up clues that I missed. Along with the head nurse, the other members of the treatment team were a joy to work with. The staff communication was vital to unit functioning and the treatment program. This highly trained group of professionals chose to work in an atmosphere that was less than ideal physically, but they brought compassion and dedication that far exceeded the norm.

Each morning we met to review each patient's progress with attention to diagnostic issues, response to medications, effectiveness of treatment approaches, family involvement, and what stage of illness the patient was experiencing. We also emphasized discharge planning and what options were available to the patient and family.

At discharge some patients would go back to their families; others would go to halfway houses or other agencies. Our social workers strove to make this a smooth transition. We did not want our patients to get lost on the streets without care. Too often when patients are discharged from hospitals without implementation of appropriate discharge and outpatient plans, the patients do not continue with their medications. They become acutely psychotic again, thus ending up back in the hospital — a cycle of readmissions that can be prevented by continued outpatient follow-up.

We had outpatient clinic every Wednesday afternoon. The inpatient staff ran the clinic. The team that had become so familiar with the patients when hospitalized also saw their patients after discharge. This clinic provided continuity of care; the staff made sure patients were taking their medications and that their living situations met their needs. The staff was also sensitive to any change in the patients' conditions. This awareness was so important to the care of our patients. Often a medication adjustment was needed to help stabilize a patient.

We endeavored to keep patients out of the hospital. Patients came to clinic every week until they were stabilized on their medications. Then appointments could be at less frequent intervals. Each week a patient came to the clinic, we celebrated a week out of the hospital. It was a time of happiness; we were all glad to see one another.

The key to the aftercare of all patients depends on several factors. Medication certainly is one of the keys, but not the only one. A place to live is so important. Often there are very few options; our social workers coordinated with community agencies to arrange the best possible solution and to ensure that our patients did not fall through the bureaucratic cracks that can create obstacles. Continued monitoring of the patient's condition is also vital in aftercare plans. A potential psychotic episode can be prevented if the early warning signs are detected soon enough. Ongoing therapy is also important for outpatient care.

The role of social workers and psychiatric nurses is crucial to outpatient care. They coordinate the entire program. Without them, there is no program, just a revolving door at the end of a hospital ward, a door where patients leave only to return again.

Just as medication is the basis of treatment within the hospital, so too it remains the foundation of outpatient treatment. With the right medication at the right dose, a patient can progress back to whatever normal is for him or her. I have seen this happen time and time again. THE MEDICATION USED TO STABILIZE THE PATIENT IS THE CRUICAL ISSUE, THE SINGLE MOST IMPORTANT CHOICE IN ALL OF TREATMENT. This emphasis was the cornerstone of our treatment.

I hope that you and your family member receive the professional care that can be provided in the right setting. As I have indicated, though, setting is not only a building. The treatment setting involves much more: the treatment team, treatment approach, services for continuity of care including discharge planning, family involvement, and follow-up programs.

6

Bipolar Disorder: A Case Study

John is thirty-three years old. He's in the emergency room of a large urban hospital. With him is his wife, Susan. She is watching John pace around the small cubicle where they are waiting to see a doctor. At random moments John stops and taps on the countertop attached to the wall of the cubicle.

For Susan the small cubicle is her last hope of finding an answer to the strange behavior John has recently displayed. Even the way he taps his hands on the counter is different from any familiar sound, the rhythm a relentless pattern that she does not understand. She cannot remember exactly how everything changed. And she has no idea what caused John's behavior, or why nothing she does seems to help him, except perhaps coming here today to this hospital. She hopes this will help.

John's problems began several weeks before that evening in the emergency room. At lunch one day, he met a guy who had this plan to make them both very rich. They were going to invest in an adaptor that would double the gas mileage of one's car. Though he had never met the man before that day, John took part of the family savings and gave the man $10,000. After that, John met the man several times, but then without leaving a trace, the man left and John could not locate him.

John did not seem troubled by the man's disappearance, instead he became consumed with the idea of the adaptor. It was on his mind all the time; it was all he talked about. His mind became so active that he could not sleep, but he didn't feel tired. He had more energy than he ever had in his whole life. He stayed up till 2 AM. Then he woke up at 5 AM and was ready to go. He was a dynamo. The ideas just poured out. He tried to write them all down, but could not write fast enough.

John did not bother about work. "Who needs a job when you're going to make a million?" John asked his wife. She could not reason with him. He would not listen. When she tried to prevent him from taking the money out of their savings, he would become angry. Fortunately, she closed the bank account before John was able to withdraw any more money.

Matters worsened quickly. There were more grandiose schemes; all centered around getting rich fast; all were unrealistic. John's speech became pressured; he could not get words out fast enough. His mind jumped from one thing to the other. He also became euphoric.

Then the voices started. John heard them and talked to them. That was when Susan knew something had to be done. The next evening she persuaded John to go to the emergency room.

John was having a full-blown psychotic episode. This was indeed an emergency. John was exhibiting the signs of mania: grandiose thinking, high energy and excitation, decreased sleep, pressured speech, active mind, flight of ideas, euphoria, poor judgment, hallucinations. He was out of control. He needed to be in the hospital.

John was evaluated in the ER by a psychiatric resident. It was quite obvious that John was psychotic. He was given 200 milligrams of Thorazine before he went to the psychiatric unit. This dose was repeated in two hours. He was given another dose two hours after that. By then John was calming down. He was not as excited. He was not as euphoric, and the voices were not as persistent. Soon he went to sleep, the first good sleep he had had for over two weeks.

John's presenting symptoms were the signs of an acute psychotic episode. He was out of touch with reality. He appeared manic. The first three doses of Thorazine really calmed him down and allowed him to sleep. He got more Thorazine the next day. This phase of the illness is known as the acute phase. Diagnosis during this phase is usually unreliable. The main goal of assessment and treatment in this phase is to help the patient through the crisis. Patients experiencing the acute phase usually respond rapidly to medications classified as major tranquilizers; another term for these medications is antipsychotics. Some specific medications in this category are Haldol, Thorazine,

Mellaril (generic name, thioridazine), and Prolixin. In John's case, Thorazine was used because of its sedating properties and fewer side effects.

Within a few days he was out of the acute phase of this illness. He no longer was grandiose; he did not have pressured speech; he was not euphoric; the voices were gone. The second phase of the illness, referred to as the post-acute phase, poses other problems. Lithium is the drug of choice for this phase, but all patients who suffer from bipolar disorder do not respond to lithium. The objectives during this phase of treatment are to prevent the recurrence of mania or depression and to enable patients to return to whatever normal living was for them. In John's case, normal living would mean going back to his family, getting his job back, returning to the life he had before he met the guy over lunch.

As John's condition continued to improve, the dosage of Thorazine was reduced. When the dosage was down to 400 milligrams a day, lithium was started. John received 300 milligrams of lithium at bedtime and 300 milligrams of lithium each morning. After several days a blood level for lithium was obtained by a laboratory test. The level was 0.4 mEq/L. The therapeutic range of lithium is 0.5 to 1.2 mEq/L. This is the level at which the medication is most beneficial to the patient. For John's lithium level to be in the therapeutic range, the dosage was gradually increased till he was receiving a daily dose of 600 milligrams of lithium in the morning and 600 milligrams of lithium at night. At this dose his blood level was 0.9 mEq/L, which is well within the therapeutic range.

John was discharged from the hospital after being hospitalized fifteen days. He was stable, showed no signs of mania and seemed ready to resume his life. John and his wife, Susan, began outpatient therapy. Both of them needed to learn about bipolar disorder and how important it was for John to stay on his medication.

Susan also needed to learn the warning signals to watch for so she would be able to tell if John was going to slip back into mania. These warning signals are as follows:

1) Problems sleeping, either going to sleep, decreased need for sleep, waking up during the night, or a combination of these sleep disturbances

2) Excessive energy
3) Grandiose thinking
4) Pressured speech
5) Overly active mind

Susan also needed to learn about depression because with bipolar disorder John could also become very depressed. Of equal importance to Susan was the emotional support provided by outpatient therapy. She had been through a terrifying experience. Her husband, almost out of the blue, had changed dramatically. His thinking was irrational. He was willing to put his family's financial future at risk, and his behavior was frightening. She felt that his anger could have led to physical harm for her. Now John was home again. Susan was shaken, uncertain, scared. Outpatient therapy was needed to help her cope with the past, present and future.

For John and all patients with bipolar disorder, there are two key issues in the post-acute treatment phase of this illness. The first is compliance. Would John take his medication? The second issue has to do with lithium. Would lithium prevent the recurrence of mania? Or would John cycle back into mania even though he took lithium? Not all patients who have bipolar disorder respond to lithium, only 60 percent do. In those cases in which patients do not respond, other alternatives are available. John's case was quite easy to diagnose. He had the signs of mania, which are symptoms of bipolar disorder. But there are different types of bipolar disorders. It is too early to tell which one John has.

Bipolar Disorders— General Statements

One half of one percent of the population suffers from bipolar disorder. The two characteristics of this illness are profound depression and profound mania. The key word is profound. Many of us have mood swings; all of us feel good from time to time. And we all have down days, times when we get depressed. Patients who suffer from bipolar disorder have profound mania and profound depression that incapacitate them.

This illness is potentially life threatening. Twenty-five percent of untreated patients commit suicide. That's right, 25 percent. This illness is often undiagnosed. It is either not recognized, or it is misdiagnosed. Patients that are in fact suffering from bipolar disorder are often diagnosed as suffering from schizophrenia. This tragic mistake means that often they are not treated correctly, and they end up being chronically ill. Thus, many patients are untreated or not treated correctly. To summarize these important issues:

Bipolar Disorder

1. Often unrecognized

2. Often misdiagnosed

3. Often untreated

4. Often not treated correctly

5. Twenty-five percent of untreated
   patients end up committing suicide

Figure 6.1

Clearly these issues need to be addressed for patients and their families.

Etiology

Bipolar disorder falls under the category of affective disorders or mood disorders. It has to do with feelings, in contrast to schizophrenia which has more to do with thinking or thought processes than feelings. The predominant features of bipolar disorder are mania and depression, which describe feelings.

For a long time we have known that affective disorders run in families. Parents who suffer from depression produce kids who suffer from depression. Parents who suffer from bipolar disorder produce kids who suffer from bipolar disorder.

Probably the most conclusive genetic evidence we have is derived from twin studies. The concordance rate in monozygotic twins (one egg twins) is over 50 percent when one twin suffers from bipolar disorder. In dizygotic twins (two egg twins) the concordance rate is only 15 percent. This rate points to the important role of genetics in this illness. If there were a strong environmental role, one would expect that the concordance rate would be a lot higher for dizygotic twins living in the same environment.

Genetic influences manifest themselves biochemically, which means that bipolar disease is in reality a brain disease. It has to do with brain chemistry that is askew or broken. The good news is brain chemistry that is broken can be fixed. We do this repair with medications that change the brain's broken chemistry.

Diagnosis

John was relatively easy to diagnose in the acute phase of his illness. Not everyone is. Though John's diagnosis was fairly easy to discern, the type of bipolar disorder from which he suffered was not readily apparent. There is more than one type; determining which type a patient has is important for effective treatment during the post-acute phase of the illness.

Diagnosis is based on three important aspects of the patient: presenting symptoms, natural history of the illness and family history. Presenting symptoms are important because these are the manifestations that bring patients to the emergency room. These symptoms are apparent, so they provide clues to determine a diagnosis. Again, when I look at presenting symptoms, I consider the following four aspects of a person: 1) mood or affect, 2) how the person thinks, 3) how he behaves or acts, and 4) how the individual perceives auditorily and visually.

The problem with presenting symptoms is that they can mislead psychiatrists who rely only on presenting symptoms for a diagnosis. That is why the natural history of the illness and family history must also be considered.

John had his first break when he was thirty-three years old. This age would be unusual for a person with schizophrenia. When a person is suffering from the symptoms of schizophrenia, the first break is usually at a younger age, generally the late teens or early twenties. This history of onset was a good clue to John's diagnosis.

In addition, John's family had a history of depression. Both his mother and sister had been diagnosed with depression. And

John's uncle was an alcoholic. Depression and alcoholism are both affective disorders. This family history suggested that John's diagnosis would be more likely categorized in the affective disorders than in schizophrenia.

Affect

Affect in Mania

Elevated mood — "high"

Euphoric

Excited

Irritable, angry

High energy

Figure 6.2

John presented in a euphoric state. His mood was elevated; he was excited, irritable, and angry. He had high energy levels and required very little sleep. These are symptoms experienced by individuals suffering from mania.

John could also go into depression, which is the flip side of mania.

In a state of depression, patients become sad; they have little or no energy, motivation or drive. Their facial expression is generally sad, and their gestures may be slow and methodi-

Affect in Depression

Sad, depressed, down

Low energy

Irritable, agitated

Figure 6.3

cal. More than likely if John had not received treatment for his illness, he would have gone into depression.

Thinking

Even though bipolar disorder is not classified as a thought disorder, patients with this illness do experience distorted thinking. In John's case, he was delusional. He had a get-rich plan that was unrealistic. He was convinced his plan could not fail and that he would be a millionaire. In other cases, I've known patients who felt they were on earth to save the universe; they believed they had been called by God for a special task and that they were the only ones who could do this.

John also experienced racing thoughts as if his mind were exploding. He could not contain all his thoughts, and as he struggled for expression, his speech became pressured.

John was also goal directed, focused, intent. When Susan challenged him, he became angry, threatening, and aggressive. She was frightened, but John was relentless and intense. If you got in his way, you could be in danger.

In addition, John's judgment was poor. He was out of touch with reality. He was so grandiose that he would have squandered all his savings on a get-rich scheme. I have known other patients who have gone to the mall and spent $3,000 on clothes or bought cars they could not afford.

Thinking in Mania

Delusional
Grandiose
Religious
Paranoid
Racing thoughts
Pressured speech
Poor judgment

Figure 6.4

Patients in the depressed cycle of this illness also have distorted thinking. Their thought process seems slower; they procrastinate and cannot make decisions. Often they feel people are against them and that the world is also against them. Life in general is overwhelming. They feel hopeless and helpless. They even have suicidal thoughts. During this time, 25 percent of untreated patients commit suicide; this depressed cycle is a dangerous time.

Thinking in Depression

Delusional
Paranoid
Hopeless, helpless
Slow
Problems concentrating
Problems with decision making
Suicidal thoughts

Figure 6.5

Behavior

John had behavior problems that are characteristic of bipolar disorders. He was up all night; he had boundless energy and was often hyperactive. He talked fast and his voice seemed to explode

Behavior in Mania

Hyper, excited
Pressured speech
No need for sleep
Very intent

Figure 6.6

from inside him. Both the pace of his speech and his gestures seemed pressured. He was very intent, focused. He looked wild. Just by observing him, one knew something was wrong.

Behavior in Depression

Withdrawal from friends, family, job
Prolonged sleep
Decreased appetite
Procrastination
Neglectful in care of self, house, family
Suicidal

Figure 6.7

Depressed patients also have problems with behavior. They withdraw into an isolated world. They quit work, stop activities and can sleep 12-14 hours a day. They seem to be in hibernation. As their condition deteriorates, they may stop caring for themselves. They may wear dirty clothes, neglect their grooming, stop attending to their residence, disregard the needs of their kids. They can even attempt to hurt themselves.

Perception

John heard voices that were not real. Auditory hallucinations are frequently experienced by both manic and depressed patients. In depression these voices may tell the individual he

Perception in Mania and Depression

Auditory hallucinations

Visual hallucinations

Figure 6.8

is worthless. Even more serious, these voices may tell the individual to harm himself.

Patients with bipolar disorder may also have visual hallucinations. Usually visual and auditory hallucinations are associated more with schizophrenia, but this is not always the case. Formulating a diagnosis on that basis can lead to a misdiagnosis.

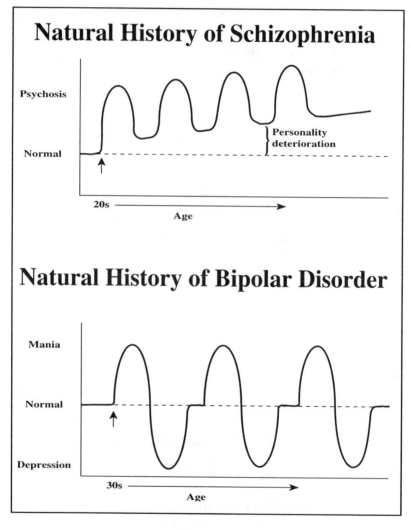

Figure 6.9

Natural History of the Illness

There are certain characteristics that are typical for bipolar disorder just as there are certain characteristics that are distinctive to schizophrenia. Patients who suffer from schizophrenia usually have their first psychotic break in their early twenties. Patients who suffer from bipolar disorders usually have their first psychotic break in their early thirties. The graph in Figure 6.9 compares the natural histories of bipolar disorder and schizophrenia.

Patients with bipolar disorder suffer from the highs of mania and the lows of depression; they cycle in and out of depression and mania with times of relative normalcy in between. During these in-between periods, these patients feel better and generally function well. Figure 6.9 depicts these cycles.

Usually patients who suffer from schizophrenia do not have mood swings. They usually do not experience normal living either. Frequently they have personality deterioration, which is the inability of a person to function adequately enough to live a normal life. These patients usually cannot work or go to school or live independently. Bipolar patients do not usually show this personality deterioration.

Family History

Family history is the third important aspect of diagnosis. Usually families with a history of affective disorders have children who may have affective disorders. Had John been in his early twenties when he had his first break, I would have thought more about schizophrenia as a possible diagnosis. But even if that earlier onset had occurred in his case, the family history of affective disorders would have led me to a diagnosis of bipolar disorder.

The real diagnostic issue is between bipolar disorder and schizophrenia, and this issue remains a diagnostic dilemma. Many patients who suffer from bipolar disorder are diagnosed as suffering from schizophrenia during their first psychotic episode, especially if that first episode comes in their early twenties.

There is hope for patients however. Psychiatrists are diagnosing bipolar disorder more frequently now. That is good news because accurate diagnosis affects treatment. Patients' families are becoming more informed. They are playing more of a role in the diagnostic process. They are learning what to tell the psychiatrist; they have a greater awareness of what information is helpful and significant. All of these developments have an important bearing on the diagnostic process. And what contributes to accurate diagnosis ultimately contributes to more effective treatment for patients.

Types of Bipolar Disorders

More than one type of bipolar disorder exists. At this time four different disorders have been identified. Categorizing the different disorders is helpful. By identifying the different disorders we can also separate patients into these different groups based on the symptoms the patients experience. Separating patients into these groups is helpful in determining the most effective treatment. We are learning that all patients who suffer from bipolar disorder do not respond to treatment in the same way.

A. Classic Bipolar Disorder

The classic bipolar pattern is one where the patient cycles into mania and then depression less than four times a year. This pattern is depicted in Figure 6.10.

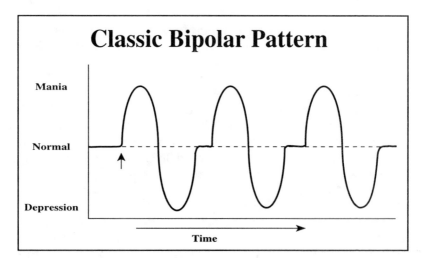

Figure 6.10

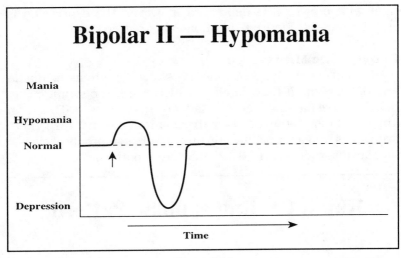

Figure 6.11

B. Bipolar II

Patients with this type of bipolar disorder show signs of depression, but the mania is not full-blown mania, rather it is of lesser intensity and is known as hypomania. This means the patient's symptoms of mania are not as prominent as a patient with classic bipolar disorder would experience. When the pa-

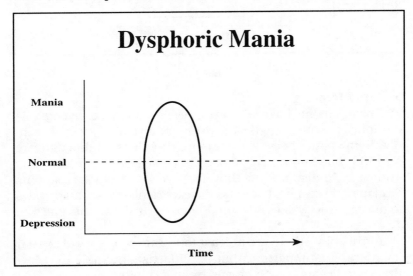

Figure 6.12

tient with bipolar II is depressed, however, the depression is very prominent. Figure 6.11 shows this pattern.

C. Dysphoric Mania

Patients with dysphoric mania show symptoms of mania and depression at the same time. Along with the symptoms of mania, these patients also are sad, down, depressed. This is an important distinction because these patients do not respond to lithium as well as patients who suffer from symptoms of classic bipolar disorder. Figure 6.12 shows this pattern.

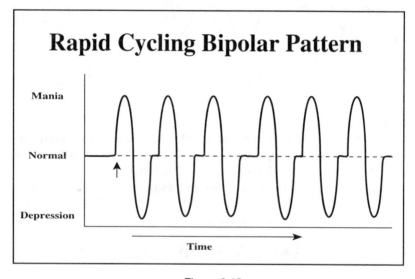

Figure 6.13

D. Rapid Cycling

These patients have at least one cycle of mania or hypomania and four or more periods of depression a year. They cycle rapidly. Some patients cycle even more rapidly than this pattern. Research has shown that most rapid cyclers are women, and studies have also shown that 18 percent of bipolar patients develop rapid cycling. Patients who experience these rapid cycles do not respond well to lithium. Figure 6.13 shows this pattern.

At this time, there are at least four different types of bipolar disorders. It is important that psychiatrists are able to recognize them because each type is treated differently.

7

Treatment: Options in Bipolar Disorders

John came through the acute phase of the illness remarkably well. Thorazine turned around the psychotic process. Now John was into the post-acute phase of the illness and there were some unanswered questions.

This episode was John's first psychotic break so we did not have much of a history of his illness before this break. In this case lithium was the medication of choice. Without a history of previous illness, certain vital questions are unanswerable at this stage: Would John cycle rapidly? Or would a different pattern emerge? Would he show dysphoria along with mania? Would he respond to lithium? Since he did not seem to have signs of dysphoria, such as an exaggerated sadness or depression with his mania, we were quite sure he was not suffering from dysphoric mania. If he had signs of dysphoria, those indications would have made a difference in what medications he would need.

John was seen in the office a few days after he was discharged from the hospital. In his first days home he had continued to do very well: he was sleeping at night, showing no racing thoughts, presenting no pressured speech, and not hearing any voices. But he felt hung over, drugged out. He was still on 400 milligrams of Thorazine at night along with 600 milligrams of lithium in the morning and at night.

Though Susan was relieved that John was improving, she was concerned that he seemed drugged out. And she was naturally still worried about all that had happened. She was still frightened; she remembered how threatening John had been.

I spent time with both John and Susan. John was taking his medication, but I could tell he was overly medicated. His mouth was dry and he looked lethargic. I reduced his Thorazine to 300 milligrams at night and maintained his lithium. John was not yet ready to return to work, although he did get back his old job. That was really important. Not working would have hurt John and also put his family into further financial difficulty.

During this first appointment, I tried to provide Susan a great deal of reassurance and support. She was in a serious situation, and she was aware of this. The role of a wife, husband or other family member is significant to the patient's treatment. Involving Susan and addressing her concerns were vital to her and to John.

Two factors are important in this phase of John's treatment. One is compliance. Would he stay on his medication? Compliance is often a problem. When patients feel drugged out, hung over, and dull, the first thing they do is stop taking their medication. I can understand that. BUT WHEN A PATIENT STOPS TAKING HIS MEDICINE, THE ACUTE PSYCHOTIC EPISODE WILL RECUR AND HOSPITALIZATION COULD AGAIN BE NECESSARY.

The other factor that is important in this phase of treatment revolves around the effectiveness of lithium. Will it prevent the recurrence of mania or the return of depression? In 60 percent of the patients, it will. But in 40 percent it probably will not. As yet I did not know if John would be a lithium responder or not. Time would tell.

I tried to impress upon Susan the importance of compliance. She had to administer John's medication until he could monitor it on his own. So far John had been compliant, but the day might come when compliance would be a problem. John would start feeling good. He would get the impression that he was well, healed, cured; he would begin to think he did not need the medication anymore, which could lead to the end of his medication compliance. The next event would be psychotic decompensation and rehospitalization.

Though I would be checking John's lithium levels for clues to John's medication habits, Susan's involvement was crucial in monitoring John's compliance and in recognizing any signs of decompensation. During John's first office appointment, I reviewed the signs of decompensation with Susan. One of the first signs is a decrease in need for sleep or a decreased amount of time a patient does sleep. This change in sleep is a real danger signal. When insomnia occurs, the patient needs to be seen immediately. This situation is an emergency; no matter what time it is, the patient needs to be seen. At this point, giving 200 milligrams of Thorazine can turn this entire process around and prevent psychotic decompensation and rehospitalization. Psychotic decompensation and rehospitalization are difficult experiences for patients and families. I try to prevent these recurrences with my patients. Recognizing the warning signals is the most effective step in turning around the cycle.

Since families often are in close contact with patients, family members need to become familiar with the warning signals, what we call signs of decompensation.

Signs of Decompensation

Not sleeping

High energy — euphoria

Racing thoughts

Pressured speech

Flight of ideas

Auditory hallucinations

Figure 7.1

Susan wanted to know these signs, and she also wanted to know more about John's illness and treatment. Would John have to be treated with medications all his life? Would he become psychotic again? Would he be able to work again? Would he ever be normal, and could the life they had once known ever be resumed? Tough questions. Bipolar illness tends to be recurrent, that is, it comes back. It is chronic.

Seventy to 85 percent of patients suffer recurrences. John would have to be on medication indefinitely. He had a chance to return to normal living, but that chance depended on his compliance and commitment to treatment. Would he take his medications and would the medications be effective for him— would they prevent mania and depression? Important questions.

John's lithium level was 0.8 mEq/L. This level is where it should be. I wanted it between 0.5 and 1.2 mEq/L. The relapse rate is lower at this range than when the level is below 0.4 mEq/L. Preventing mania is important and is more likely when the levels of lithium are in this higher range. If John stopped his medication, he had a 50 percent chance of relapse in five months.

There is another problem with recurrences of mania. I have followed patients who for one reason or another have cycled into mania and have been readmitted to the hospital for treatment. Each time they are admitted, they seem to stay in the hospital longer and their recovery does not seem to be as complete. They do not seem to respond as well to lithium in the post-acute phase of the illness. These factors make prevention of the recycling into mania even more crucial for patients and their families.

8

Alternative Treatments for Bipolar Disorder

Sixty percent of patients who suffer from bipolar disorders respond to lithium; 40 percent do not. But there are alternatives— alternatives that provide hope and opportunities for those patients who do not respond to lithium.

Betty was thirty-two when she suffered her first psychotic break. She was hospitalized and treated. After she left the hospital, she was started on lithium. She took the medication. She had a lithium level in the therapeutic range; she was monitored closely, but within six months she had another psychotic break. Again she was treated and released from the hospital. Again she was treated on lithium. In four weeks she was depressed. During the next year Betty suffered from mania or depression a combined total of seven times. She was in and out of the hospital. It was obvious that the lithium alone was not preventing the recurrence of her cycles; it just was not working.

There are two other medications that are good alternatives if lithium is not effective. In many instances Depakote and Tegretol are effective alternatives. Depakote is effective around 50 percent of the time in preventing recurrence of mania. Tegretol is effective 70 percent of the time. Both medications have been used in treating acute mania, and the percentage of cases in which they are effective is comparable to lithium's rate of 60 percent.

I started Betty on Tegretol. She received 200 milligrams twice a day for three days. I wanted to make sure she could tolerate the medication. Slowly the dose was increased to 1000 milligrams a day; I wanted to get a blood level in the therapeutic range between 7-12 µg/mL. Betty responded to Tegretol. She did not recycle into mania, however she had some bouts of mild depression.

In another patient's case, trials of both lithium and Tegretol were ineffective. When I began treating Sally she was thirty-five. She had a two-year history of cycling into mania, being rehospitalized, restarting lithium, and then going into mania again. She had been tried on Tegretol, but she just could not tolerate the medication's side effects. So I tried her on Depakote. She was started on 250 milligrams twice a day. After three days this dosage was increased to four times a day, then gradually up to a dose of 1500 milligrams a day. This dose was effective. Sally did not cycle into mania any longer. She had a blood level in the therapeutic range.

At times lithium and Tegretol or lithium and Depakote must be used in combination to prevent the recurrence of mania. When any one of the drugs, the lithium, the Tegretol or Depakote, is discontinued, the mania returns. The goal, of course, is to maintain patients on the fewest medications possible. I know of one case where a patient was started on lithium and cycled into mania. Tegretol was then added. Again the patient cycled into mania. Then Depakote was added. The cycles stopped. When Tegretol was discontinued, the cycles started up again. This happened when Depakote was stopped also. This particular patient needed lithium, Depakote, and Tegretol. This case was unusual, but it gives us still another alternative.

Side Effects

These medications are classified as anticonvulsant medications; at one time they were primarily used in the treatment of seizure disorders. In the last twenty years, though, their actions have been proven effective in other conditions, such as bipolar disorders. The anticonvulsants are important medications that are of benefit to many patients, but as with all medications, they do have side effects. Sedation is one of the side effects first experienced by patients on these medications. Usually the feeling of sedation goes away within time. Tremors of the fingers may also occur, as can nausea.

Depakote can cause severe, sometimes fatal, liver problems. Liver function tests should be obtained when symptoms of anorexia, jaundice, nausea, and lethargy occur. Studies of the serum liver enzymes, SGOT and SGPT, are helpful. Also increases in serum billirubin would be cause for concern.

In the past, a few patients on Tegretol, approximately one in ten thousand, developed aplastic anemia or agranulocytosis. This occurrence has been rare and is in fact declining further. Monitoring the patient's complete blood cell count by means of a standard laboratory test will detect aplastic anemia, especially when associated with a fever. Agranulocytosis can be fatal. Medications are discontinued when white blood cell counts fall below 3000.

Overall, these medications are considerably safe when monitored closely. For many patients they provide a viable alternative to lithium. The patient and his family in conjuction with the patient's psychiatrist need to consider both the potential side effects and benefits of each medication.

Clozaril, the antipsychotic that is so successful in treating schizophrenia, has also been helpful in both treating mania and preventing its recurrence. Clozaril needs close monitoring with weekly white blood cell counts. Three percent of patients on Clozaril develop bone marrow suppression, agranulocytosis, which can be fatal, but also can be prevented by close monitoring.

The existence of these alternative treatments has provided options that are necessary for patients who do not respond to lithium. Without these alternatives, a pattern of recycling and rehospitalization becomes all too prevalent. With these medications, this pattern can potentially be controlled; patients and their families can look forward to effective treatment and increased stability in their lives.

9

Depression: A Treatment Dilemma

Lithium can be successful in preventing manic cycles, but patients can also cycle into depression. Depression is a real problem; patients feel sad, have difficulty concentrating, lack motivation, lose energy and interests— in general they feel life just is not fun anymore, and they no longer experience joy in living.

Depression is a serious problem that calls for treatment. Medications used for the treatment of depression are generally referred to as antidepressants, however there are different types of antidepressant medications. They are classified according to their mechanism of action, which means that different medications work in different ways to bring about chemical changes within the patient's brain. By changing the chemistry, these medications are effective in alleviating the patient's depression.

The three categories of antidepressant medications are the tricyclic antidepressants, monoamine oxidase inhibitors (commonly referred to as MAOIs), and serotonin reuptake inhibitors. The problem in treating depression with these medications is the possibility that they can induce mania. The rate of cycling into mania while using tricyclic antidepressants is around 25 percent. The MAOIs can cause mania 12 to 21 percent of the time. However, in a controlled study with Prozac, a serotonin reuptake inhibitor, mania did not occur.

In addition to these medications, lithium is also effective in treating depression. Electroconvulsive therapy, ECT, is also useful in treating depression in patients suffering from bipolar illness. Some patients become profoundly depressed and may even have psychotic features. They can also be suicidal. ECT works faster than medications and is often very useful in treating depression. It can be used in acute mania as well. At times manic patients are so psychotic that they need rapid intervention. This intervention is especially warrented when the mania is so extreme that it becomes life threatening.

ECT causes convulsions by sending electric currents through the brain. Prior to the procedure, patients are anesthetized and a muscle relaxer is given to prevent injury during the convulsion. Modern ECT is a safe, effective way to treat depression and mania.

Psychopharmacology, which is the use of medicine to change brain chemistry, can get very complicated in bipolar disorder. I try to approach this very systematically. Treating the acute phase is straightforward. Patients usually respond to conventional antipsychotics, such as Thorazine. They also respond to Depakote and lithium in the acute phase.

During the post-acute phase, treatment can get more complicated, especially since bipolar disorders are life-long illnesses. In addition there is a group of patients who do not respond to lithium. This group includes patients with less severe mania, dysphoric or mixed mania, and rapid cycling patients.

There is also a group of patients who have responded well to lithium for five to fifteen years; THEN THEY CHOOSE TO DISCONTINUE THEIR TREATMENT AND SUBSEQUENTLY SUFFER A RELAPSE. When restarted on lithium, these patients do not respond to it, which may mean that lithium may not be as effective once it is discontinued. This ineffectiveness emphasizes the point that patients need to stay on lithium throughout their life if lithium has been effective. THE NOTION OF STOPPING AND THEN RESTARTING LITHIUM IS PERILOUS, BECAUSE THE MEDICATION MAY NOT BE EFFECTIVE AGAIN. Bipolar disorders are life-long illnesses; stopping lithium may interfere with its effectiveness. As with other life-long illnesses, the key is ongoing, effective treatment.

In 1975 I had a patient who was admitted to our psychiatric unit. He was acutely psychotic. In a few days, he was out of the acute phase of the illness and we tried him on lithium. He responded. He even went back to school that summer. Things went very well for several months, but then he started having symptoms of a psychotic episode. He had problems sleeping, had excess energy, and began to hear voices. He was admitted to another hospital, and the lithium was discontinued by the physician treating him. He was treated with antipsychotic medications, which are effective in acute psychotic episodes. Within a few weeks, he was stabilized and was discharged. Soon after discharge, though, he went into a vegetative state, completely withdrawn. His family brought him back to our unit. I restarted him on lithium, but he did not respond to it this time. Although he was able to go home after fifteen days, he dropped out of school, and spent most of his time in his room at his mother's house. He lost what he had gained while on lithium; it would have been better if he had remained on it. To see that potential lost is frustrating to me, but that frustration is only a fraction of what I know the patients and families experience.

This case is just one of many in which medication issues were complicated. Often I create a life chart of the history of my patients' illnesses and treatment. This life chart is somewhat like a time line; it provides a visual way to help me keep things straight and uncomplicated. The chart on this page is an example of a life chart. You can see that when carbamazepine was added in 1988 the mania cycles were eliminated. Depression remained a problem until 1991 when the use of the antidepressant medication Prozac was effective in treating this depression. This type of chart keeps treatment issues focused;

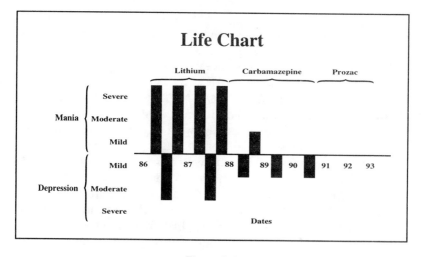

Figure 9.1

with the chart one can tell which medications were effective and which ones were not.

The objectives are to keep patients out of mania or depression, and to provide them the opportunity of living as normal a life as possible. I feel strongly that the goals of living independently, working, and being involved in family relationships are all realistic. Treatment with these medications is a life-long process. We know that. Bipolar disorders are chronic and recurring. That is why there is more to treatment than medications.

Biological factors predominate these illnesses, but the manifestations are behavioral and psychological changes. These changes are evident in the patients' attitudes, perceptions, personality, moods, and thinking. These changes can be devastating.

Psychological intervention can be of great value to patients, spouses, and families. When asked, patients will say that therapy is important for them. Patients can be helped in group, individual, and family therapy.

The establishment of a good therapeutic relationship between the biological psychiatrist and the patient is very important. Sometimes this relationship can be hard to accomplish and it takes time. Though medication evaluations usually can be done in about fifteen minutes, a good therapeutic relationship requires effort, but goes a long way in increasing the likelihood of medication compliance. A significant relationship develops over time.

I feel that a team approach is most beneficial. At the University of Louisville, social workers and nurses played key roles in creating a therapeutic team approach. They provided support and education to patients and their families.

To ensure that vital information is available to patients and their families, a variety of resources needs to be available. Pamphlets, videotapes, classes, and support groups all are vital in providing education on these illnesses. Access to this information increases patients' and families' awareness. Often this increased awareness will make a significant difference in recognizing changes in a patient's condition. Increased awareness can thus help ensure that treatment is adjusted to meet the changes in the patient's condition. Increased awareness can also contribute to medication compliance. With education, patients and families understand that these illnesses are chronic in nature. Though the chronic nature of these illnesses initially seems overwhelming, understanding that these are life-long illnesses helps patients and families make important decisions about treatment.

Social workers should meet with family members on a regular basis. In John's case, Susan needed the kind of support that could be provided by this regular contact. She met with our social worker every week. This meeting was very helpful to her especially in the first weeks after John was discharged. That period of transition can be particularly stressful to family members. What might happen next? Is the patient safe at home? Are the children safe? How can you reach help when you need it?

Susan was also involved in therapy with John. They had to learn to live with John's illness. Issues— difficult ones— had to be voiced and discussed. For instance, John had to learn that Susan wasn't against him. He did not want her hovering over him, but on the other hand, she was frightened and felt she needed to protect him and the family. Family therapy helped both of them deal with these issues.

John was also involved in group therapy with other patients who suffered from bipolar disorders. The group therapy sessions were led by a social worker. The group met every week, and together the patients talked about what was going on in their lives. They talked about their medications and how they felt about taking them. They discussed what was going on in their families and how their relationships to their spouses and children were affected by their illness. They talked about jobs, how difficult it could be to find and maintain employment. Some of the patients lived with their biological families; some lived alone. They all helped each other, supported each other, and learned about their illness together. The social workers who led this group were very astute in recognizing early signs of depression or mania. Psychiatric help was just a phone call away.

Social workers are also involved in another aspect of treatment, which is to arrange appropriate living accommodations for patients. Often patients cannot live with their families. They are unable to go back to their biological families, or they may be separated or divorced from their spouses. These arrangements present problems. Social workers who are aware of community resources can provide vital links between patients and these resources. Ideally, social workers can assist patients in finding residence in halfway houses or apartments. Unfortunately, most communities do not have enough of these residences available. There is a desperate need for more halfway houses and community-based living resources.

I rely heavily on social workers. Without them the system can quickly break down, and patients are the ones who suffer most from such a breakdown. We know that family therapy can help manic patients take lithium, prevent relapse, and improve verbal communication within family relationships. Spouses fear recurrences, feel helpless, and may resort to denial. These very real, natural human responses can be dealt with in family therapy. Patients involved in group and family therapy are hospitalized less frequently. I look at success from the standpoint of preventing mania or depression, keeping patients out of the hospital, and monitoring how the medications work. Often I lose sight of the long-term goals vital to the patients: living independently, working, maintaining relationships with families, living normally. Patients live with different criteria for success. They live with daily disappointments and failures. They live with mood swings, maybe not as bad as before, but present nevertheless. They put up with side effects of medications; they sometimes feel drugged out, dull. They fight hard to concentrate and to stay motivated. These struggles persist for patients and their families.

I need the help of a treatment team in caring for these patients. I need social workers and nurses. Unfortunately, as a psychiatrist in private practice, I do not have a team like that, though I can consult with social workers and nurses. But treatment teams can be found in medical schools, community mental health centers, and state and local hospitals.

One other key component of treatment is political involvement. All of us — families, friends, patients — need to be politically active. We need to join local and national organizations that work hard in this arena, organizations that are advocates for the mentally ill. The National Alliance for the Mentally Ill, NAMI, does this, as does The National Depressive and Manic-Depressive Association. Political action is one way to ensure that research will be funded and that good public care will be available.

The public sector, one in which I have been active for fourteen years, frustrates me. Just recently I met with the director and the medical director of a community mental health center. We talked about issues of diagnosis including the use of lithium and other medications. We discussed Clozaril, which the community mental health center was not using to any extent. These concepts were foreign to them. These directors acted as though they had never before heard of or thought of using alternative medications. This closed-mindedness is frustrating, to say the least. I am sure I did not handle the situation very well either. There are better ways to deal with that lack of awareness. We all need to work to treat patients more effectively. We can put political pressure on legislators. We must. Too many lives are being wasted in our present system. We can do more, and we can do it better.

10
Schizoaffective Disorder

Diagnosis has always been a basic problem in separating bipolar disorder from schizophrenia. At one time schizophrenia was an all-inclusive category. Almost everyone who had a psychotic break ended up with that diagnosis. Bipolar disorder was just the opposite. It was very narrow in diagnostic scope. If you had paranoid ideations or heard voices, you were excluded from a bipolar disorder diagnosis. You could have all the other symptoms of bipolar disorder, but if you had any of the so-called symptoms of schizophrenia, you could not be suffering from bipolar illness.

This diagnostic approach got us into trouble not only from the diagnostic standpoint, but also in terms of treatment. For some reason, treating schizophrenia with lithium was something one just did not do as a psychiatrist, or at least most of us did not.

In the late 1940s and 1950s, Dr. John Cade in Australia reported on the effectiveness of lithium in treating patients suffering from bipolar disorder. He also reported on five patients diagnosed as suffering from schizophrenia; Dr. Cade used lithium to treat these patients. Prior to the introduction of lithium, these patients had been restrained constantly, but after starting lithium, these patients improved to the point where they no longer needed restraints.

With the introduction of lithium as a way of treating these chronic and devastating illnesses, we had a medication that allowed a person to regain some normalcy in his/her life. Here was a medication that took away some of the symptoms that led to chronicity. Bipolar patients who responded to lithium did not exhibit the withdrawal, inertia, and lack of motivation that one often found in patients suffering from chronic illnesses. These negative symptoms are so disruptive of a patient's normal life. They rob patients of the very core of life.

Could lithium be effective in mental illnesses other than bipolar disorder? Cade's study demonstrated that lithium had helped some patients suffering from schizophrenia. What were the clues to this effectiveness? Could some presenting symptoms or family histories help us in this dilemma? Were we missing lithium responders? Were there patients who suffered from some of the symptoms of schizophrenia and some of the symptoms of bipolar disorder? If so, did this call for a new diagnostic category and further study of treatment approaches for these patients? From these questions our understanding of schizoaffective disorder developed.

We had staff meetings every morning on the psychiatric unit at the University of Louisville. Social workers, nurses, chaplains, psychiatric interns and residents, medical students, and students from various other disciplines attended. We went over the diagnosis, treatment, and prognosis of each patient every day. We questioned our diagnosis of a patient repeatedly. Were we missing something? Were we treating the patient with the right kind of medication?

We looked at presenting symptoms. Were there signs of mania? Excitement? Euphoria? Grandiosity? Increased energy and no need for sleep? Were there any signs of depression, anger, aggressive behavior? What did the family history show? Alcoholism? Depression? What about the natural history of the illness? Did the patient experience any normal living between acute psychotic episodes? These questions were addressed again and again.

Let me tell you about a patient, Robert. When Robert was twenty-nine years old, he developed psychotic symptoms. He came to the emergency room at our hospital. Robert presented with symptoms of a psychotic break and was admitted to the psychiatric unit. He heard voices, saw faces, was paranoid; he was out of touch with reality. He was somewhat typical of patients suffering from the symptoms of schizophrenia. He was treated for these psychotic symptoms and was almost out of the acute phase of the illness when one of the social workers discovered that Robert's mother and aunt had histories of depression. In addition, Robert had an uncle who suffered from alcoholism. Both depression and alcoholism are affective disorders. The medical students on the team stated that Robert had done quite well in college; he was a music major and played the violin in the symphony orchestra before his first psychotic break. I diagnosed him as suffering from schizoaffective disorder and started him on lithium.

The recovery was remarkable. The hallucinations went away. So did the paranoia. Robert picked up his violin again, returned to his profession, and went back to school that summer. The turn around was dramatic. Later that fall, some of the psychotic symptoms broke through. Robert became paranoid again; the voices came back; he had problems sleeping. He ended up in the emergency room and was readmitted to the psychiatric unit. We treated him with Thorazine; he came out of the acute phase of the illness and was again stabilized on lithium. He did well. Nine months later, the same thing happened. This time Robert was seen at another hospital. He was diagnosed as suffering from the symptoms of paranoid schizophrenia and taken off lithium. He stopped going to school and quit playing his violin. He moved back in with his mother.

Had Robert not responded to lithium? His symptoms did break through on occasion, but were easily handled with the addition of Thorazine. I have treated many patients out of the hospital with this same approach. In two or three days they returned to normal and functioned remarkably well. I ran into Robert's mother several years later and found out Robert was still living at home, in a back bedroom, not doing much, chronically disabled. Sad story.

In the seventies and eighties, I directed a research program at the University of Lousiville. Through the research program we developed an experimental approach to treating patients suffering from schizophrenia. Patients came from across the country. David, a young man from Boston, had the "classic" symptoms of patients who suffer from the symptoms of schizophrenia. He qualified for the research study that had strict diagnostic criteria. I thought David suffered from schizophrenia. His mother had also been diagnosed as suffering from schizophrenia and had been treated for many years. David was paranoid, heard voices, had a blunted, flat affect, and suffered from the personality deterioration that goes along with the illness.

He responded extremely well to the experimental protocol. His symptoms left and he looked good. His family was pleased.

Then he was hospitalized for a physical illness. He had to drop out of the experimental program. His symptoms returned. While waiting to get back into the program, David was started on lithium. He responded. He did much better. His symptoms went away again. After three or four months, David and his dad left Louisville to go back home. He was doing well when he left and was to be followed by a psychiatrist at a very well-known institution in Boston. To my surprise, David was taken off lithium. He went back into the chronic state that he had presented when I first saw him.

From this experience and others like it, I learned that I could not separate out lithium responders from non-responders on the basis of presenting symptoms. Often I saw patients who I felt were suffering from the symptoms of schizophrenia respond to lithium, Tegretol, or Depakote, or combinations of these medications. As time went on, almost all of the patients that ended up on our ward were started on one of these medications. I could not separate lithium responders from non-responders through the diagnostic methods that we utilized. Everyone was tried on lithium or the anticonvulsive medications. This became standard procedure. Some patients did not respond, but some did. When they did respond, their lives were turned around. Many were able to live productive lives. Some went back to work; others went back to school. They were able to live independently.

This approach makes sense to me. Yet most community mental health programs, most state hospitals, most hospitals with acute short-term psychiatric units do not try patients on lithium or anticonvulsants. There is even a reluctance to do this in the psychiatry departments of major medical schools around the country. I am not sure why. Maybe we still think that we can separate patients suffering from schizophrenia from those suffering from schizoaffective disorder or those suffering from bipolar disorders. Maybe we still think we can tell who will respond to lithium and who will not. I do not think we can. I cannot; I am sure of that. How many patients are there who would respond to lithium, Tegretol, or Depakote if tried on these medications? One hundred thousand, two hundred thousand, three hundred thousand? I do not know. What I do know is that patients need to be tried on these medications.

If we just looked at the economic savings, medication trials for these patients would be worth pursuing. There is, however, more than economic savings. Patients can get their lives back; parents can get their kids back.

Is there such a disorder as schizoaffective illness? Should we form this diagnostic category? Yes, we should. If it just shifted patients out of the diagnostic category of schizophrenia, that would be worth a lot. But it does more than that. It forces psychiatrists to look at treatment alternatives. It makes us re-evaluate patients when they are diagnosed as suffering from schizophrenia, and that re-evaluation can change their lives. Patients suffer from the effects of a chronic mental illness, but they also suffer from the stigma that society still puts on schizophrenia. Families still suffer guilt from this stigma. Parents still blame themselves. I am glad we are not making the diagnosis of schizophrenia as often as we once did. Using the category of schizoaffective illness enables us to accomplish this goal.

For patients diagnosed with schizoaffective illness, their treatment is divided into acute and post-acute treatment. Earlier we discussed how the goals of treatment are different depending on the phase of the illness. With schizoaffective illness, I treat the acute phase the same way that I treat any acute psychotic episode, I use Thorazine. Other antipsychotics work as well. For me lithium is the medication of choice in the post-acute phase of schizoaffective disorders. If patients' psychotic symptoms break through on occasion, then they can be easily treated with antipsychotic medications until the symptoms go away. Lithium helped Robert live a relatively normal life between these psychotic symptom breakthroughs. He should have been maintained on lithium. Certainly Depakote and Tegretol deserve trials in patients who do not respond to lithium. Some patients respond to these medications alone or in combination with each other. One patient needed all three medications for stabilization. This medication trial is worth trying. It could be the difference between functioning and not functioning very well.

How do we as professionals and family members approach these illnesses? I need to learn all I can about these illnesses. I need to read, listen, and ask questions. Knowledge is so important. As a psychiatrist, I must be good at diagnosing, the best I can be. I need help, all the help I can get. I need informed, knowledgeable family members who know what to look for, what symptoms are important, what family history makes a difference, and what is significant about the life history of the illness. You, as a family member, can help me make a more accurate diagnosis by just being informed.

Laboratory studies and x-rays may also be important. EEGs and MRIs can also help in diagnosis. A good physical examination provides information. Psychological testing can be helpful. I would insist on a good workup of my family member.

Where do you find this approach? I would go to a psychiatrist who is biologically oriented, a biological psychiatrist. One place that I would go to find a biological psychiatrist is a medical school. They are there. I would call the department of psychiatry and find out if they have a program that diagnoses and treats these illnesses. Many large cities have medical schools. There are two or three in each state. In some areas, state hospitals and community mental health centers are connected to the medical school. Maryland has an example of that design — the state hospitals are connected to the medical schools' departments of psychiatry. North Carolina has a similar program. Other states are also developing these programs.

Join NAMI. Become politically active. It is the only way that funds will be supplied to carry on research programs. It is the only way community mental health centers and state hospitals will receive adequate support.

11
Issues of Living

Once a patient is ready for discharge from the hospital, the problems of living and functioning in the world become a primary focus. Many patients choose to live with their parents, but this choice may have serious ramifications for the patient and family. Sooner or later the parents may not be able to care for the patient. The parents' own health and financial status needs to be considered. The fact that the adult patient may outlive his parents is also a reality that must be faced. If the parents die, what happens to the patient?

Aside from these issues, there are emotional considerations. An adult child living with parents creates many problems. Parents may feel guilty and sad; they may also feel angry and resentful. So, too, the children experience these emotions.

In view of these problems, the likelihood of parents and their adult children living together harmoniously is very rare. Yet, over 50 percent of all patients diagnosed as suffering from the symptoms of schizophrenia live with their parents. Most of these families live together because they do not have any alternative. This is clearly not a very beneficial arrangement. Could a more effective solution be found?

In Louisville, Kentucky, during the mid-1980s, a group of individuals sought a more effective solution. These individuals who were involved in the field of psychiatry worked together and were able to rent a house in the downtown area of Louisville. It was one of those spacious old houses that grace the older neighborhoods of cities, a great house that with renovation became a home for patients who needed a place where they could live as independently as possible. A professional staff

83

was hired; social workers played a particularly key role in coordinating the program. As time went on, a second large house and then apartments were added. Patients progressed from a supervised halfway house with a lot of staff to apartments that were unsupervised. Some patients were able to work. This increased level of functioning was beneficial to them. Some patients never moved out of the halfway house because their condition necessitated closer supervision. Nonetheless, they too were more independent than they would have been living at home with parents.

Today patients live in these facilities, but unfortunately there are not enough facilities to meet the needs of all patients. It takes dedicated staff with vision to develop and keep these facilities available for patients. Much hard work is involved, but it can be done. I have seen these facilities succeed and have seen the benefits to the patient, family and community.

Patients who come to these facilities learn to function in ways that are essential for everyday living. These patients may have been out of touch with reality; some have been that way for years. To function they must be incorporated into society, actually into life itself, into independence. They have to learn how to live more independently as time goes on. How do you live with other people in close contact? How do you work out differences? Who does the dishes, cleans up the place, takes out the trash? Then there's getting a job, just getting there on time, doing a good job, being consistent, dependable. So much has to be relearned or learned for the first time. The process of re-entry takes time.

I remember Jane, a young lady that came to us in the mid-seventies from California. She had been hospitalized seventeen times and she was only nineteen years old. She responded well to a research treatment protocol, but her re-entry process was a long, difficult road. She came to the halfway house. With the structure and assistance provided there, she began preparing to attend college. At first she took only a few classes, but as time went on, she enrolled full-time. She graduated from nursing school and went on to earn a Master's Degree in Nursing. Today she is married with a family and works in an intensive care unit.

From her first day in the halfway house, Jane was involved in group therapy and program activities to promote her reentry to society. Two things were very important for Jane's progress. First, her treatment was effective; second, she had the personal drive to go through the re-entry process. Our treatment team provided the program; she provided the determination and drive to learn and gain independence.

Part of Jane's determination to gain independence involved acceptance of her need for medication. Probably the most difficult struggle that must be confronted is the issue of medication compliance. Patients do not like medication. Medications have side effects that cause some patients to feel tired, hung over, drugged out. Because of these feelings, some patients decide not to take their medication. Other patients do not like feeling they need the medication. Whatever the reason for noncompliance, studies show that when patients quit taking their medication, they decompensate, become psychotic and need rehospitalization.

One of the many positive things about lithium is that it has few bothersome side effects. All medications need to be monitored. Patients on lithium need blood levels checked frequently during the stabilization period and then every six months or so. Monitoring ensures that patients are in the therapeutic range for lithium and not in the toxic range. It is also important to monitor Tegretol and Depakote blood levels for the same reasons. With the more conventional antipsychotics, bothersome side effects can become a problem. Use of those medications with their side effects can increase the problem of patient noncompliance.

More often than not in my practice, I have dealt with the issue of noncompliance by using the medication Prolixin Decanoate. This is a long-acting antipsychotic medication that is given by injection every two to four weeks. Use of this medication is beneficial for those patients who do not comply with daily medication regimens. By administering a long-acting injectable medication, I know the patient is getting the medication he/she needs.

For patients who do not comply with their medications, and even for some who do, medication dosages may need to be adjusted. This is why consistent outpatient follow-up is important. When I see patients who are having trouble sleeping, I am immediately alerted. These patients may need their medication adjusted to prevent decompensation. Signs of decompensation include the following: problems going to sleep and/or staying asleep, hyperactivity, paranoia, hearing or seeing things, affect that is blunted, flat, excited, angry or aggressive. These are all clues to decompensation.

At the University of Louisville, frequent contact by our team of social workers and nurses prevented many patients from decompensation. The key is frequent contact and prompt response to signs of decompensation.

In view of these many issues of living, one can understand that the treatment process is complex and involves more than prescribing medication. The goal of helping patients live to their maximum potential needs to be kept in mind always. Unless this goal is continually pursued, we allow patients just to vegetate when there are other viable alternatives for them.

12

Coping with Mental Illness in the Family

When one family member suffers with mental illness, all family members are affected. I remember when I was a young boy, my Aunt Jose's illness affected our entire family. Since childhood Jose had suffered from epilepsy. Over the years she was increasingly incapacitated to the point where she had to rely on my grandmother for care and support. Whenever my parents and I went to visit, Jose sat off to herself in the room with us or alone in her own room. I remember she always looked different, and acted in a way that seemed strange to me as a child who did not yet understand her illness.

At times my parents offered to have Jose come stay with us, but this offer was always preceded by worry, tension and even arguments between my parents. Where would Jose stay? What if she had one of her "spells"? Could we manage her?

Usually our offers were declined, but eventually Jose's condition deteriorated to the point where my grandmother could no longer provide for her safety and well-being at home. So Jose was sent up North to the state hospital.

All this happened before my sixth birthday. Now as an adult, I can only envision what Jose's life was like all those years in the state hospital where she eventually died. And I can only imagine the inner turmoil my grandmother and parents went through trying to deal with this illness. All the family shared in the suffering. Though Jose endured the most, I believe my grandmother also felt the pain as deeply as if she were Jose. My grandmother was getting older; she was a widow coping daily with the uncertainty of the future. Most importantly, Jose was her child; watching her child suffer must have been a deep sadness to endure.

All of us have hopes for our children — expectations and dreams for their lives. When we are confronted with illness, often out of the blue and with no warning, a period of denial can seem a safe haven. Eventually parents of children with mental illness come face to face with the undeniable reality of their child's illness. When this confrontation occurs, a period of questioning and searching often begins.

The first steps involve seeking help. An accurate diagnosis from a biological psychiatrist is essential. Once a diagnosis is made and treatment implemented, other feelings and concerns may arise. Many questions are asked: "Will my son or daughter get better? What did I, what did we, do wrong? How can we help? Why did this happen to our child, to us?" All of these questions and intense feelings are part of learning to cope with a child's illness.

Or suppose the family member is your spouse, someone with whom you have chosen to share your future, someone who may also be the father or mother of your children. Feelings of abandonment, loss, loneliness, worry, resentment may surface all at once or slowly over time. If children are involved, then their insecurities and fears can be overwhelming. How can you help them understand a problem you may not be able to accept yourself?

Whether the family member is your child or your spouse, your parent, sister, or brother, the illness affects family members at many levels. Responses may vary depending on the family relationships, past experiences, and a vast number of other influences. The overall impact, though, is generally one of shock, and at times helplessness. In some moments hope may seem very far away.

During these moments and all through the many experiences a family may encounter, two issues are vital to remember: 1) the more information you have regarding your family member's illness, the more you may be able to help him or her, as well as yourself and the family, cope with the illness; 2) though professional help is necessary, the patient and family have the right to be part of the treatment plans.

To explain further these vital issues, the next sections will explore in detail the following aspects of family involvement:

choosing treatment, creating a supportive environment, under-standing the concept of least restrictive treatment settings and the implications of hospitalization, and finding ways to meet the challenges to carry on with your life.

13

Choosing Treatment

The decision to seek treatment for your loved one is the most difficult step. You may have been raised to believe time will heal all, or you may feel there is something more you could or should do that will "fix" the situation. Perhaps your loved one is ambivalent regarding treatment and fluctuates between helplessness and resistance. Seeking help may conflict with deep personal values of privacy and self-sufficiency.

These are important issues that I respect. Seeking treatment, however, need not deny the concerns you and your family member feel. On the contrary, seeking treatment will be the first step toward regaining a focus and direction that will ensure the individual, confidential, and quality care you value.

Once you have reached the decision to seek help or to assist your family member in seeking help, the next step is where to look for that help. You may pursue many paths from the yellow pages of your phone book to recommendations by friends, family physicians, ministers, community referral sources, etc. The appendix of this book includes names and addresses of organizations that may assist you in securing treatment resources.

Whichever path you pursue, you need to ask vital questions and investigate information to make the final selection. Though the field of psychiatry and mental health treatment encompasses a vast array of services for a wide variety of conditions, the illnesses that we are considering in this book are those which affect brain chemistry. Bipolar disorder, schizophrenia, and schizoaffective disorders are genetic illnesses that require medical treatments. Medications are an essential first step. Psychiatrists are the only mental health professionals who can prescribe medication, so treatment starts here. Psychiatrists can be in private practice or affiliated with hospitals, clinics, medical schools or community agencies.

When you talk with a psychiatrist, you have a right to ask questions. Certain information is crucial for you to decide whether this psychiatrist is right for your family member. The following is a list of questions to discuss with the psychiatrist:

1) What is your treatment approach or your philosophy of treatment?
2) How do you determine if medication is necessary?
3) Do you prescribe medications, and if so, how do you determine which medications are indicated?
4) Are there any medications which you feel are particularly helpful? Which ones? Do you use lithium? Depakote? Tegretol?
5) Are there new medications, such as Clozaril, which you will recommend if indicated?
6) Are you available during an emergency, and if so, how can you be reached?
7) How often will you see my family member?
8) What contact will you have with the family?
9) If hospitalization is necessary, to which hospital do you admit your patients?
10) Are you involved with day care centers, partial hospitalization programs, halfway houses?
11) Do you recommend additional services as indicated, such as family therapy, etc.?
12) How do I contact you for additional information?

You may have additional questions that are of particular concern to you and your family member. The crucial issue is to ask for the information you need to know. Without answers you can not make an informed decision or choose the treatment that is in the best interest of your loved one.

14

Long-Term Care

Schizophrenia, bipolar disorders, and schizoaffective illnesses are long-term, chronic illnesses. They last a lifetime. Care must continue for a lifetime. Families need to have long-range plans. Every member of the family needs to be considered in the plan. Families often are concerned that their loved one may not be getting the best care that he or she can receive.

I feel that the best evaluations for seriously ill patients are done at medical schools. Frequently this evaluation can be done on an outpatient basis. There are two or three medical schools in each state. They are usually found in large cities or in cities where there are universities. You need to find biologically oriented psychiatrists. This is essential. Not only do you want a thorough evaluation, you also want treatment recommendations. It is well worth the cost to go to the Department of Psychiatry at a medical school. They may require a physician referral, but often a phone call to the outpatient clinic of the department is all you need.

Biologically oriented psychiatrists are in private practice in communities throughout the country. How can you find one in your community? First talk with your family physician; he or she will probably know a biologically oriented psychiatrist. Or you can contact your local NAMI chapter, which provides information about psychiatrists in the community. If you can not locate your local NAMI chapter, write or call NAMI at the locations listed in this book's appendix, and the representatives can direct you to the chapter nearest you.

Once you have information on a psychiatrist, I recommend you schedule an appointment and ask questions about his or her treatment approach. In chapter 13 I listed questions that I consider important for you to ask. The answers to those questions will help you know whether this psychiatrist can help you and your loved one. I would ask a psychiatrist about his treatment ideas. Does he prescribe lithium, Depakote, Tegretol? How about Clozaril? You may have to hunt around to find a psychiatrist who is biologically oriented and will prescribe the medications needed. Finding one is well worth the search; finding a biologically oriented psychiatrist could make all the difference in the world.

Every city has community mental health centers. They are listed in the phone book. My experience with these has been mixed. I am usually very impressed with the social workers and nurses, but not so impressed with the psychiatrists. I have had the same experiences at the state hospitals with which I have been associated. You must talk to the psychiatrists in these settings. You need to go to them informed about the illness and about your loved one. You need to know your family history and the natural history of the illness in your family member along with the presenting symptoms. The more you know, the more you can help in the diagnosis and treatment of your loved one. Go prepared.

In deciding whether a treatment facility meets your needs, I want to recommend one caveat: Looks can be deceiving. The trend in health care settings is toward buildings and designs that are eye catching. True enough, environment can establish a safe, harmonious atmosphere for treatment. Lavish attention to external surroundings, however, can reflect a focus on public image more than on quality patient care. What's essential is to look beyond the exterior and become familiar with the program and people involved in implementing the program. You can become familiar by asking questions, observing, and seeking recommendations from community resources such as NAMI, your church, your family physician, and community support groups.

Let me tell you about two of my experiences which highlight ways that looks can be deceiving. Our hospital in Louisville was an old inner city hospital. Though it met all safety standards, it did not look good. Every effort was made to keep it clean and bright, but those efforts could not erase the fact it appeared downtrodden. The years had taken their toll, but a patient could get great care there. The staff was committed to the hospital and cared for the well-being of patients. The staff members could have abandoned ship and gone to one of the newer, fancier facilities, but they did not. A family spirit of dedication and compassion prevailed, and this spirit was evident in the quality care patients received.

By contrast, in the late 1970s I was asked to do a consult at a very expensive, very prestigious hospital on the East Coast. I was impressed with the place, which was situated on expansive, attractive grounds. The buildings were well-kept; the food was good. The care, however, was below standard. The patient I saw had been there since the 1950s and was not given medication for her condition. She was delusional, withdrawn, blatantly psychotic. A social worker told me, rather indignantly, "We never force medication on our patients." I replied that it did not make much sense to allow a psychotic woman to choose to live in a psychotic state without attempting to force the issue of medication and its potential benefits. When my patient was properly medicated, she did much better.

Needless to say, I was not very impressed with that place. Despite all the modern conveniences and luxuries, the treatment was static. I kept going back to see that patient; I also kept expressing my opinions and concerns.

Do not be fooled by private hospitals in nice buildings. Care is not always the best there, and it is very expensive. Get to know the psychiatrist and staff wherever your loved one receives care. There are good psychiatrists and staff in many different settings. You just need to find them.

15

Providing a Supportive Environment

Perhaps one of the most difficult challenges families face is the daily struggle to provide a supportive environment. How does a family create such an environment? What are the factors or conditions that establish this atmosphere? The answers may vary depending on the family and patient, but one fundamental principle applies to all families: minimizing stress is essential. To do so may seem impossible at times, especially when family members are in the midst of coping with the daily challenges of chronic illness. But there are specific steps families can take that will help keep stress to a minimum for their loved one and for themselves.

We first need to review why patients with mental illness are particularly vulnerable to stress. Due to the characteristics of their illness, they are unable to deal with stress effectively. These characteristics include the following: 1) acute sensitivity to sensory overload, 2) impairment of ability to concentrate and focus attention, 3) unpredictable, sometimes strange and frightening perceptions, 4) fluctuating, intense and unpredictable moods, 5) feelings of helplessness, incompetence and dependence, 6) difficulty with accepting mental illness and the limitations/implications it imposes on life. In view of these characteristics, the need for reducing exposure to stress becomes apparent. Furthermore, research has proven that a correlation exists between high stress levels and psychotic decompensation.

Given these factors and the high level of stress you may be experiencing, what can you do? There may be days you feel overwhelmed and frustrated, incapable of coping yourself, much less helping someone else. Those are normal, understandable responses to the extremely difficult situation you are experiencing. One of the most important steps you can take is caring for yourself. Chapter 19 provides specific resources you may find helpful.

In addition to the all-important process of caring for yourself, there are ways you can create an atmosphere conducive to meeting the daily challenges mental illness imposes on you and the patient. One of the most basic and important steps a family can take is to establish a quiet, calm, consistent environment. Too much noise, too much activity, too many people — all of these can be confusing to the patient who cannot filter incoming stimuli.

Throughout any given day, people are bombarded with a variety of sounds, sights, smells, feelings; generally they can sort through these to focus on what is relevant and to ignore the rest. Patients with mental illness, however, cannot focus or sort effectively and thus can easily be overloaded by these sounds, sights, etc. Sensory overload can be present on a day-to-day basis and even more so at festive times such as holidays, family reunions, and parties. Preparing for these events by providing quiet space and time for the patient will benefit both the family and patient.

Consistency is also important in maintaining a supportive environment. Providing predictable routines and schedules can be reassuring to patients. Change affects us all, and for patients and family members, mental illness brings many changes. Establishing a daily pattern that provides both consistency and flexibilty can minimize the effects of change and uncertainty. Stability and predictability give one control over one's life. For patients whose inward stability is lacking, outward stability becomes even more crucial.

In addition to the external environment, families can provide a supportive atmosphere by the way in which they communicate with the patient. Frequently patients suffering with mental illness are acutely sensitive to tone of voice and can be vulnerabie to paranoia, mistrust, and misinterpretation. Families who pay special attention to selection of words and tone of voice are helping the patient in ways that are not always visible, but are definitely meaningful. In times of stress, controlling your inner feelings can be difficult. What is easier to control is how you project those feelings — what words you choose, what tone of voice you project. Clear, simple statements help patients understand what is being conveyed to them. Sometimes the message may need to be repeated. You may need to ask the patient to verify that the message that he or she received is the same one you intended to convey. These extra steps will help promote understanding.

Communication also involves dealing with conflicts. Miscommunication can be especially troublesome for the family. Loving another human being inevitably involves disagreements and conflicts as part of the process of understanding. And when the person is someone with a mental illness, the conflicts can be frequent, intense and unresolved. The primary factor is recognizing which conflicts are of real significance and which can be deferred or ignored. Some issues may require the assistance of a professional or the guidance of a support group. What is essential to remember is that you have choices in dealing with conflicts. You have choices concerning which conflicts to handle, when to address them, how to approach them, and where to go for help. As much as possible, family members need to work together rather than in isolation or opposition to one another. Often this cooperation is extremely difficult, and participation in a family support group can be vital to the family's health as well as to the patient's.

All these strategies are fundamental to the issue of helping the patient develop confidence. There are some things patients with these illnesses can do and some they may find impossible or overwhelming. Knowing what a patient can and cannot do is very important for all people involved with the patient. What patients can and cannot do varies from patient to patient and may vary over time. Discovering what are realistic expectations for the patient is an ongoing process. As a concerned and involved family member, you want to be both realistic and encouraging. The balance between accepting patients' limitations and encouraging their efforts is sometimes a precarious one, but it is a vital and worthwhile balance for families and patients.

Often the family's encouragement helps the patient develop confidence. At the same time, a family's awareness of limitations can help the patient feel positive about what he or she can achieve, even if it is less than what he or she attempted. Setting short-term goals can be a foundation upon which to build. Simple things need to be accomplished before more complex endeavors can be attained.

With the discovery and use of medications, such as Clozaril and lithium, patients are being relieved of the negative symptoms that were so common among patients suffering from schizophrenia and other severe forms of mental illnesses. Increasingly these medications are opening doors for patients, doors that lead to enhanced functioning and improved life styles. I am very optimistic about the future. Many patients with these illnesses will be able to live more normal lives. There is hope.

Yet we must always remember that patients need to come to terms with their illness so they can experience the best possible future available to them. Many patients try to deny their illness; they want to believe they are no different than anyone else. They want to believe they are not chronically ill or that the illness they experience can somehow magically disappear. They stop taking their medication; they decompensate; they require hospitalization to help them stabilize their lives again.

From my experience patients will believe what they want about their illness, but what is crucial is their awareness that treatment is necessary. The issue of medication compliance is of utmost significance to the patient and family. In most families when the patient stops taking prescribed medication, the results are devastating. Very few families can cope with this situation; the toll is too great, the risks too dangerous.

To achieve patient compliance with prescribed medication often requires diligent attention by the family and psychiatrist. Appointments with the psychiatrist may need to be increased or varied to enhance patient's acceptance. Medication schedules may need to be reviewed and revised to meet patient needs. In some instances patients can receive medications that are long acting and thus are required less frequently. Though compliance is an ongoing challenge, facing this challenge is vital to the patient and family. With the combined efforts of the family, psychiatrist, support groups, and other health care professionals, the challenge can be met.

In dealing with compliance issues, family members may experience many different emotions from fear to guilt to doubt and hopelessness. At times they may also want to believe a magic wand can make all the problems go away. Throughout each day, week, month, year, families facing the pain of chronic illness experience many intense emotions. These emotions may affect the family's decisions, behaviors, relationships, and work. What's important to remember again and again is that you are not to blame for the illness your loved one is experiencing, and that you have a responsibility to yourself. Stay informed about treatment. Do all that you can to help your loved one, but also take care of yourself. Be willing to acknowledge that you may need help and support to meet the challenges you are facing. The next chapters explore a variety of resources available to families who are searching for ways to deal with their challenges and to carry on with their lives.

16

Crisis Situations

Day-to-day dilemmas require attention and problem solving approaches that can be implemented gradually. Problems that are crisis situations, however, do not afford us the time to implement a solution gradually. Action is required and usually urgently. Some crises can be prevented; some cannot. Regardless, all crisis situations require prompt attention.

Families can face many different crises. The following are ones that I consider most critical for families coping with mental illness: 1) medication compliance, 2) psychotic decompensation, 3) violence and aggression, and 4) suicidal behavior.

Medication Compliance

We have looked at the benefits of medicine. These benefits end if the patient stops taking the medicine. This is a serious problem. If a patient refuses to take medication, he or she will probably become psychotic and need hospitalization. Even though a patient is psychotic or becoming psychotic, you cannot force a person to take medicine. Standing by while this noncompliance happens is difficult. You feel helpless.

During the past ten or so years, the courts have passed laws that make treating patients against their will very difficult. These laws were designed as protective measures, but in many cases the end result lets a psychotic person choose his or her destiny. Often they choose wrong, and often families must make very difficult decisions regarding medication compliance.

In my family I would insist on medication compliance. I say this realizing that insisting on compliance might cause a no-win situation with alternatives that are not very good. If you insist, your loved one may leave and be in danger. If you don't insist, your loved one and your family may be in danger as the acute symptoms of illness recur.

One of the most helpful approaches is to work with the patient's psychiatrist to find the medications that cause the fewest side effects for the patient. Some patients also prefer the long-acting medications, such as Decanoate, which can be administered by injection once every two to three weeks. The issue of taking medication daily is no longer a problem with the long-acting injectable medications.

With the availability of Clozaril, the problem of compliance has been altered. Patients are not bothered by many side effects when they are on this medication. Clozaril is well tolerated, and enables patients to feel better. Clozaril treats the negative symptoms of schizophrenia much better than the more conventional antipsychotics. I have had no compliance problems with my patients on Clozaril. Risperdal also has good potential for compliance. I think it will be a useful medication because of its user-friendliness. Medications such as these are helping patients and families deal with the issue of medication compliance.

Acute Psychotic Episode

Patients do decompensate and become psychotic. This situation is an emergency. Often this decompensation happens when a patient does not comply with medication. Though it can occur when a patient takes the prescribed medication and the psychotic symptoms just break through; more often than not, decompensation is a compliance problem.

The first sign of decompensation is sleep loss. Patients cannot get to sleep; they roam around at night and get their nights and days mixed up. When I learn about a patient's sleeplessness, my red flag goes up. A psychiatrist can stop the whole process of decompensation at this stage by aggressive treatment.

I remember a night when the mother of one of my patients, Robert, called. I could hear the fear and uncertainty in her voice as she told me her son was up half the night for several nights in a row. While the rest of the family slept, Robert watched television or roamed about the house as though he were lost. Robert's mother knew from past experience that this sleeplessness meant trouble.

After her phone call, I saw Robert within the hour. When a patient's family calls and reports sleeplessness, this situation is an emergency. Robert came to my office, and his appearance and behavior confirmed what his mother feared.

Robert's sleeplessness was the first sign of decompensation. The voices he had heard in the past were now returning, and he conveyed paranoid ideation. Robert needed to have this process turned around, so I started him on 200 milligrams of Thorazine at supper and 400 milligrams at 10 PM. Robert went home, and I was going to see him again the next day. His mother had my home phone number and knew she could reach me any time she needed.

The next morning Robert told me he had slept better. He looked better also. He took the Thorazine again that day and came back to see me the following day. This routine continued for five days. Over the weekend Robert's mother called. He was sleeping better, and his condition continued to improve.

On the sixth day, Robert came for an appointment and he definitely looked better. His sleep was stabilized; the voices had diminished, and his paranoia was gone. But he was over-sedated and talked of feeling "hungover" from the medication. The Thorazine was decreased to 400 milligrams at bedtime. After several days it was reduced to 200 milligrams and within a short time, discontinued.

During the entire episode, Robert remained on his lithium and Stelazine. The Thorazine was just added to his other medication. On this medication combination, Robert improved, so I was able to keep him out of the hospital. I could do this because Robert was compliant with his medication, and his mother picked up the early signs of decompensation. I could also trust her to call me if the situation got out of hand or if she needed help. These circumstances are not true for every patient, but they are for many. When they are, the patient and family come through a crisis situation without the painful ordeal of rehospitalization.

Violence and Aggression

Sometimes patients become aggressive and assaultive. This behavior usually happens during an acute psychotic episode. They may intimidate, threaten, or even assault a family member. Aggression cannot be tolerated; it can be dangerous. A plan needs to be developed to deal with emergencies of this nature. Here are some questions that are important: 1) Is the patient having a psychotic episode? Are voices telling him to hurt someone? Is he paranoid? In this case, professional help is needed immediately. You need to contact a psychiatrist or take the patient to the hospital. At times it may be necessary to seek assistance from the police, especially if you feel the patient is dangerous. 2) Is this a confrontation, or is the person angry for another reason? Will dealing with the reasons defuse the anger, or is the patient out of control and dangerous? Dangerousness is the real key. If the patient is dangerous to himself or others, he needs help — you have to act.

Most states have laws that will allow involuntary hospitalization if a patient is dangerous to himself or others, or if the patient is in an acute psychotic state. At times families need to get a court order to commit a patient.

Make sure you know in advance whom to call if the situation warrants involvement of the courts. Your local community mental health centers usually have this information. Have a plan; be prepared. Hopefully, you will never have to involve the courts, but be ready.

Needless to say, you must remain calm during these situations. Calmness goes a long way in stabilizing a situation.

In hospitals when situations get out of hand, the staff can call security guards or additional personnel. The presence of these individuals can convey both security and commitment to maintaining patient safety. Know where you can turn for help: neighbors, family members, your community emergency services, whatever is available. Know how to call for help when you need it; have a plan that you can enact.

Crucial to your plan is communication with the family member who suffers from mental illness. Make sure you convey what cannot and will not be tolerated. Do not allow intimidation or threats to begin. Preparation and communication will help prevent violence and aggression.

Without such preventive measures, property can be damaged and people can be hurt; the patient and family may face the painful experiences brought on by violence.

Suicidal Behavior

Suicidal behavior is both a psychiatric and a medical emergency. The suicide rate among chronically mentally ill patients is high. Patients also threaten suicide; sometimes these threats are real, but in some cases they may be manipulation, a way to get attention. Knowing which threats are real and which are manipulation is difficult, if not impossible. When a patient talks about suicide, take him or her seriously.

Most state laws will allow patients to be hospitalized involuntarily if they are dangerous to themselves. Many families are reluctant to take out a court order on their loved one. This decision is difficult, but one that at times is necessary. There is a lot of guilt connected with this decision. Patients remember and are resentful, but their safety is an important issue. There are some behaviors that cannot be tolerated. Decide what they are in advance of the situation. Be willing to act if the situation calls for it. I feel there are two issues that may require a court order for involuntary hospitalization: 1) dangerousness to others, 2) dangerousness to self.

We have discussed the issue of patients' aggression and violence directed to other people. Sometimes a patient's dangerous behavior is directed both to others and to himself or herself. The newspapers report the tragedies that result from these cases. The warning signs of potentially dangerous behavior may be evident when we examine these cases closely.

Often suicide and depression go together. Patients suffering from schizophrenia can also become depressed. Depression is a danger signal. Dangerous behavior can be more than just suicidal ideation. Patients can be so delusional that they act in dangerous ways; for example, they may believe they can walk down the middle of a busy freeway and not be harmed. These cases, as well as the cases of suicidal ideation, are cases in which the patients may be treated against their will. Know whether the laws in your state allow patients to be treated against their will and under what circumstances. Be aware of the ways to obtain such treatment should it become necessary.

I am often asked, "What can families do?" My answer is that families do the best they can. Families can only do so much. They become exhausted. They need a break from time to time. When the situation becomes intolerable, when family life is threatened, when parents are being driven apart, then decisions need to be made.

Bill and Mary had a son, Frank, who was diagnosed as suffering from the symptoms of schizophrenia. Frank controlled the family on matters ranging from the details of daily life to the plans for special events. When a vacation was planned, Frank decompensated. Bill wanted to hospitalize Frank, but Mary did not. She felt that they should change plans, stay home, stand by their son. This pattern happened almost any time Bill and Mary planned to get away. Frank did not want them to go. Usually they did not go. Bill wanted Frank in a research program. Mary did not; she did not want Frank on Clozaril; she did not want him to have blood tests every week. Over time Bill and Mary's relationship broke down. They could not agree about Frank. They were frustrated, angry, and exhausted. Once while talking with me at my office, Bill said, "There are days when I wish Frank would step in front of a truck. Then this hell would be over." In his heart Bill did not want his son to die, but at that moment the family anguish was overwhelming. Bill was sad all the time, Mary was also. Their relationship was gone, eroded by their son's illness.

Parents need to work together as a unit. If they are driven apart, then everything deteriorates. Families need stability; parents need to come to agreement, compromise together. Talking helps, information helps, and support groups help. The families and people you meet in support groups share what they have learned; support groups can be a valuable resource for a family trying to deal with chronic illness and to work together as a family.

There usually are other children in the family. They suffer also. They need parents who are together, unified. Work on it; the spousal relationship is the most important one in the family. Seek ways to strengthen the family unit; find a support group. They are in most every community; you find them with NAMI, in churches, hospitals. Take the time to find one. I do not see how families survive without these groups and the support they offer.

17

Problem Solving, Setting Limits

Lowering stress certainly cuts down on the incidence of psychotic breaks, but it does not eliminate all problems. Despite lowering stress, the patient's behavior can become abusive. Home life can become unpleasant. Families learn to tolerate a lot of unacceptable behavior while struggling to set limits.

Families can usually come up with a long list of behaviors that are tolerated but cause concern. They range from noncompliance with medication to hostile, aggressive behavior. At the heart of these problems is a basic question: Should there be rules and regulations that govern an adult child living in the home of his or her parents? Yes, I think so. There have to be.

The next question centers around what the rules are, what they cover. If there's a rule for everything, then life gets to be overwhelming, burdensome, and oppressive. If there are no rules, then everyone suffers and families are disrupted. The list of behavior problems is long; the issues may vary from one family to another. Areas of concern often include the following: refusal to take medication, poor hygiene, argumentativeness, messy rooms, constant tardiness, heavy smoking, bad table manners, and manipulative behavior. The list could go on and on. Some of the issues are not that important to certain families; other issues are of great importance. Each family has to choose what is really important and focus on those issues.

Skills in Problem Solving

All of us learned problem-solving skills in school, but we often do not realize what steps we go through to solve problems. Here is a list of steps to basic problem solving:
1) State the problem
2) List the possible solutions
3) Choose the best solution
4) Carry out the solution
5) Evaluate the results

Step 1: State the problem

Family members have a right to control their own households. They need to feel safe, have private time, have possessions that are their own, and feel that they have control over what happens in their home. These expectations are not unrealistic. I have the right to have control over what goes on in my house. I should not feel guilty about this right. Are there issues that are so important that if they are not solved, other living arrangements must be considered? Yes. It depends on the family and what it can tolerate. One essential issue for me would be medication compliance. I would demand compliance. Other families may have other issues.

I think that it is helpful to make a list of problems and then decide which ones need immediate attention. The temptation is to go after them all at the same time. This lack of prioritizing can become overwhelming and end in frustration.

So many of these problems center around power and control issues. An adult son or daughter wants to be in control of his or her own life. To begin with, suffering from these illnesses robs them of much of this control. Now they live with parents who want to control them also. This struggle is analogous to the one that occurs in adolescence — kids want to be free, parents want to protect them. But the difference is that now the struggle is between parents and an adult child. All of us want to have some control over our lives, or at least have the feeling that we do. Being mentally ill does not take away that desire.

Let me tell you about John and his family. John moved back in with his parents after independent living arrangements had been unsuccessful. He suffered from the symptoms of schizophrenia. At first his parents were relieved that John was home; they could provide the support and assistance they hoped would help him. As the months passed, though, tension began to grow. A variety of daily conflicts occurred, most often involving John's room. John never made his bed, let his clothes pile up on the floor, and often let dirty dishes and trash accumulate for days. Things were never in order. Big deal? To some families, maybe not, but John's parents valued order in their lives.

One solution is just to close the door. Out of sight, out of mind. My mom would not have been able to live with that. She could see behind the door. I have three daughters; when they were teenagers and their rooms were a mess, I just closed the door.

Several questions need to be asked: Can John clean up his room? Does he have the skills for that task? Cleaning up a room takes a degree of organization, some motivation, some energy. One has to be persistent. This consistency may be too much for John to handle. It may be easier to straighten John's room every week for him than to be in constant conflict over it.

There are multiple solutions to a specific problem. One solution is for us to change our minds about the problem. Perhaps it is really not that big of a deal. Maybe all that's needed is to close the door. On the other hand, different families have different needs and values. What seems a simple solution to one may not solve the problem for another family. The key issue is to consider a variety of solutions and decide what is most realistic. Can John's parents identify certain tasks John can do? Can the family reach a level of order they can accept and John can maintain? Compromise and flexibility are crucial elements of problem solving.

Step 2: List the possible solutions

A list of solutions is helpful. There should be several. They should be discussed. Flexibility is the key to problem solving. In John's case, the door could be closed. John's messy room might then be tolerated. Or a list of specific things to clean up could be made, and a family member could help John.

Each family will determine its own list based on the problems and needs. This list can be like a map that provides direction; a list can point out the many different routes that are available to reach a destination.

Step 3: Choose the best solution

This step sounds easy, but may be difficult. Certainly, the choice will not be the same in each family. The solution should be a family decision with everyone involved, if that is possible. Sometimes it is not possible to come to an agreement. When that happens, parents have the right to make choices about what the people living in their home do. Parents need to be in control. Often parents are forced into decisions that are hard for them. They feel guilty when they demand things. They should not. Demands need to be made; structure needs to be maintained, or everything breaks down.

Sounds easy, but it is not always so. What seems simple may be complex. At least, choose a solution. Work at it; agree on it; compromise when necessary. Be concrete, specific. Make sure everyone understands the solution, and then begin to implement it. That is the only way you can have order.

Step 4: Carry out the solution

A solution demands action; it must be carried out. The family member must be given a clear, concise statement of what is expected of him. Now John may resist this. He may state that his room is his room and that he should have control over it, that there needs to be some place that is his, where he alone is in control. These arguments need to be resisted. Parents cannot be manipulated into a guilt trip at this time. There must be consequences for the family member, if the solution is not carried out within reason. Arguments should be avoided; opposition should be handled directly with no negotiation after a plan is formulated. Families should not be put on the defensive about their decision.

Step 5: Evaluate the results

How are things going? Has the plan worked? Do we need a new approach? A different solution? Time answers these questions, but follow-through is necessary. If there is no follow-up, there is no bite in the rules, no motivation to carry out the plan.

What I am suggesting in this chapter is challenging. The principles are simple but carrying them out is quite difficult. Barry lived with his family. He had a history of not taking his medication. When he stopped taking his medicine, he became psychotic and had to be hospitalized. After three or four weeks of hospitalization, Barry was discharged. He was stabilized on his medication and was doing well. Barry and his parents came to my office to discuss where he would live. Barry wanted to go home again. I told his parents that the one stipulation I would make as a parent was that Barry had to stay on his medication or he would not be allowed to live at home. Things went well for a few months. Barry stayed on his medication. Then, he skipped a follow-up appointment, and consequently ran out of his medicine. His parents were aware of what was going on and they made Barry leave home. He went to a halfway house to live. Without medication, Barry started showing signs of psychotic decompensation. He could not sleep at night; he became paranoid; he heard voices again. One morning at 3 AM, there was a knock at his parent's door. There stood Barry, cold, wet, and wanting to come home. His mom let him in. Later, we talked about this situation, when Barry and his parents came to my office. The solution seemed quite simple to me — Barry should not have been allowed to return. He made the choice not to take his medication. His mom lamented, "What's a mother to do?" Here was her son, cold, wet, decompensating, standing there. The solution was easy for me, but I am not Barry's mom. What is a mother to do? The very best she can do under very difficult circumstances.

18

The Role of the Family in Rehabilitation

Families play a major role in rehabilitation. This is true for a number of reasons. Resources for outpatient rehabilitation are scarce. Halfway houses are scarce. Partial hospitalization programs are not available. Long waiting lists for rehab services exist. The time families are together, therefore, can be very valuable; a lot of resocialization can go on in the daily life of a family. Families often find ways that help sons and daughters become more competent and grow in independence.

Rehabilitation starts with correct diagnosis and correct medication. It may even start before that, with knowledge. Knowing about and understanding all you can about an illness goes a long way in ensuring a correct diagnosis and proper medication. These illnesses are brain diseases; the brain's chemistry is broken. The only way the brain's chemistry can be fixed is with proper medication.

There have been so many advances in diagnosing, yet patients are still misdiagnosed. Why misdiagnosis still occurs seems incredulous to me, but it happens. There have been so many advances in the area of psychopharmacology, advances such as the use of lithium, Tegretol, Depakote, and now Clozaril and Risperdal. Patients should be on the medication that works for them, but they are not. What a tragedy. Do not let this happen to your loved one. Be informed, read, go to conferences, ask questions. You, the family members, are the ones who can make sure your loved one is properly diagnosed and gets proper medication.

Ned's mom and dad were in my office before Christmas. Ned's mom looked at me with tears in her eyes and said, "We have our son back for Christmas." I was so thankful that Ned was on the right medication for him, finally. Now Ned is back in school and his improvement continues.

When patients get on the correct medication, they lose the negative symptoms of the illness. They are not as withdrawn; they can concentrate; they have energy; they are motivated. They are willing to make social contact, to get out more, and to do things. Ned was not in a rehabilitation program. He did not have the benefit of trained rehabilitation therapists structuring his day, but he was resocialized. This process was successful for many reasons. A great deal of credit goes to his family, but not all of my patients respond like Ned.

At the University of Louisville, rehabilitation was a treatment priority. I wish we had more programs to facilitate rehabilitation. As patients' negative symptoms abate with proper medication, their interest and potential for rehabilitation increase. We need more programs to help patients realize this potential.

Rehabilitation should center on a person's strengths. For example, Mary was a young woman whose strength was tennis. She was first diagnosed with schizophrenia in her twenties. Before her illness she was a ranked tennis player in Kentucky. It seemed natural for her to be involved in tennis again when the negative symptoms of schizophrenia melted away. She responded to this plan. Early success led to more success. She found new friends on the tennis court. She learned she could do something well again — she could still hit a forehand, and she could still play tennis. Friends led to other activities. Mary was bright; she was a good student in a private high school. After she graduated from high school, she went to college and earned a Master's Degree in English. Mary's family provided her emotional support throughout her rehabilitation. Mary was also in a rehabilitation program for over a year. She worked hard getting her life back together.

Mary's family worked with her, helped her, and encouraged her. They knew her strengths, her past success. They involved her in tennis, in school. They pushed her, got her involved; they helped her overcome her reluctance to try.

What are the strengths of your loved ones? Sports? Studies? Music? Art? Perhaps they are now ready to get involved with these activities again. Help them; encourage them; enable them. The process may be slow and at times painstaking, but do what you can; do whatever is necessary to get them involved again.

Motivation

Motivation is, and has been, a problem. Motivating patients to participate in some activity is so important. Just get them started at something: volunteering for a charity, doing some chores around the house, or taking a class. Just doing somthing is so hard, yet so necessary for rehabilitation. Parents can help motivate sons and daughters in these activities.

Lack of motivation is part of the negative symptom complex of patients suffering from the symptoms of schizophrenia, schizoaffective illness, or bipolar disorder. We now have medications that deal with negative symptoms. Lithium did this for Ned. Clozaril did this for John. Tegretol did this for Robert. Should families have expectations for their loved ones? Sure, but they should be realistic. If negative symptoms persist, motivation will be down. Everyone becomes frustrated when expectations are not realistic. Demands produce anxiety. Anxiety is not all bad. All of us have been motivated by it from time to time. The danger is producing too much anxiety. This has the opposite effect that we want. Too much anxiety immobilizes.

Independent Living

The goal for any patient is independent living: an apartment, a job, the ability to live and carry on the business of taking care of oneself. Independence requires knowing how to dress, how to take care of grooming and appearance, how to hold down a job. It also requires knowing how to manage an apartment, how to handle money, how to interact socially and develop friendships. Independent living means knowing how to make it in the real world. All these abilities require know-how, learning experience, and encouragement.

Social skills can be learned. Most of us learn these skills in childhood and adolescence; in adulthood we refine them as we mature. Patients may have learned these skills too, but their illness may necessitate learning them again, or in some cases for the first time. Treatment programs need to incorporate social skills. At the University of Louisville we spent time with patients; we played volleyball, had supper together, sang songs, talked, went to the mall, just got together to share time. All these activities helped patients develop social skills and confidence. We encouraged patients to go to church, join clubs, get out with other people. Involvement in group therapy can also be helpful, just the interaction with others is important. These things build up our patients' confidence. This confidence is essential to the process of rehabilitation. I can remember great times at my house — we had cook-outs with patients and staff; we played guitar and sang songs. One of my patients could play and sing really well, and she led us. Many of the patients in that group in the late seventies and early eighties are now living independently. They work and support themselves. This achievement is not something that is out of the question. One young lady has a Master's Degree in English; another has a Master's in nursing and is married and works in a hospital. Another young lady has a job and lives independently. I have kept in touch with some of these patients. There are five others who were doing well ten years ago, and I feel are still doing well. These are not unusual cases. This independence and success can be accomplished. These goals are realistic.

Families want to know if their loved ones will ever experience joy, independence, a future that is not always tarnished by illness. Yes, patients can be rehabilitated; it is a reality. I have seen it happen.

I have kept in touch with many of my patients from the University of Louisville. They continue to do well, participating in life rather than being trapped by the negative symptoms of illness. These patients' achievements are not unrealistic. Fortunately, these achievements are reality for these patients, and they can be reality for your loved one too.

19
Community Resources

There are resources in the community; I feel that care there is improving. Some community facilities are very good, some are not. You have to check them out. Patients are usually assigned a therapist or case manager. In most instances, case managers are social workers or psychiatric nurses. Case managers know what is available in the community and can help patients and their families find the needed services.

Case Management

A case manager coordinates the services a patient will need. Most patients need multiple services. The system is often very complex. It is easy to fall between the cracks. Patients have a great deal of difficulty dealing with the various agencies. Often separate agencies are involved with the same patients. When I was medical director of a state hospital, I coordinated the social workers at the state hospital and the community mental health centers. I knew whether patients were showing up for their appointments and taking their medications. We kept close track of them. There was less rehospitalization because of this monitoring and coordination of services.

Case managers can be of great help to patients and their families, and families need to be in close contact with the case managers. Communication is crucial. Families need to inform the case manager when a patient is not taking his medication, is having difficulty sleeping or is showing other signs of psychotic decompensation. Case managers need to know if patients are drinking, taking drugs, or misusing their medications. If patients are not showing up for their appointments, then case managers need to be informed. Get to know your loved one's case manager. Know how to contact the case manager. The system is complex; case managers know the system and can be a great help.

Supervised Living Facilities

I think most patients should live in supervised living facilities rather than with their biological families. Families often feel guilty when they make arrangements for their loved ones to live in a supervised living facility, but to me this arrangement makes the most sense. I have not seen too many families that function very well when they have adult children with chronic illnesses living with them. The strain and conflict are just too great.

In Louisville, Kentucky, we started such a facility in 1983. At first it was a halfway house. Then a second house was added. These were well supervised. Then apartments were added that went from moderate supervision to minimal supervision. Patients who could, progressed through the system. We also tried to get jobs for our patients. For some, a job was a very positive progressive step towards independence.

Not all communities have supervised living facilities. You need to find out where the facilities are and look them over. Supervision and cost are important issues to consider.

Community Mental Health Centers

Community mental health centers (CMHC) are found in almost all communities. They are government funded, but patients may be charged a fee on a sliding scale for services.

Again, there are good centers and bad centers. The basic problem over the years has been the struggle for power and control between psychiatrists, psychologists and mental health boards. Many psychiatrists have left CMHCs because of this struggle. They grew tired of being voted down on important issues. For me the issues centered around treatment. At times my patients were taken off their medications when they went to the outpatient clinic after being discharged from the hospital. Without their medication, the patients became psychotic and ended up in the hospital again. I stopped that cycle by setting up our own follow-up clinic to make sure patients remained on their medications.

When CMHCs and state hospitals connect with the department of psychiatry at a university medical center, this type of power struggle does not persist. It makes sense that psychiatrists are in control of basic treatment plans because they are the only mental health professionals that can prescribe medications. The decision for medication is not to be voted on or altered by non-psychiatrists.

The real advantage of a CMHC is that it is set up to provide comprehensive care. As a physician, I cannot provide this for my patients. I do not have a case manager, social worker, or nurse. I do not have a day care program, partial hospitalization, or stabilization unit.

Social workers and nurses provide assistance in all these areas. They can coordinate the treatment of patients, which prevents patients from getting lost in the system.

Patients and families need education and support geared to the situations they face with chronic illness. Social workers and nurses provide this support. Social workers guide patients toward valuable community services, job training, supervised living arrangements, and socialization groups. Nurses can administer medication, check medication levels and coordinate completion of necessary laboratory tests. I have found social workers and nurses to be informed, concerned mental health professionals. They are the backbone of CMHCs and state hospitals. They provide real care and concern for patients and families.

Potentially, the CMHCs provide the most comprehensive and best care for patients. Potentially. Be sure to evaluate the CMHC in your area. It could provide real help to you in the form of day or respite care, partial hospitalization, or acute stabilization. Political pressure needs to be applied to ensure that communities have good CMHCs. NAMI applies that kind of pressure. Join your local organization. Be active.

General Hospitals

Often there are psychiatric units in general hospitals. Some of these units are run by CMHCs; some are connected to medical schools; some are run by private psychiatrists. These are acute, short-term units. Patients are treated aggressively with medication and then discharged. The average length of hospitalization has been ten days. I would advise a family to determine the costs and what kind of payment plans the hospital accepts.

There is some concern that short stays are not very helpful for patients. Studies have shown that there is really no difference between short stays and long stays from the standpoint of rehospitalization and prognosis. Short stays can be just as effective in many situations and certainly do not foster hospital dependence as much as long stays do. They also cost less, a big factor in mental health budgets.

State Hospitals

State hospitals get a lot of bad press. Not all of them deserve this evaluation. In the 1960s, state hospitals were decentralized. The decentralization plan sought to return patients to their local communities for treatment at various agencies. This plan has not been completely successful. We need state hospitals. We need state hospitals that are tied to university hospitals, as they are in Maryland. University appointments attract psychiatrists to these state hospitals. It is hard to attract good psychiatrists to the state system. Teaching and research opportunites help. Better care usually comes out of this also.

Know about the various hospitals in your community. Know what to do, and where to go if an emergency situation arises. Have phone numbers available. Know whom to call.

Rehabilitation Services

Patients who suffer from severe illnesses often have impairment even when symptoms are controlled by medication. Patients who suffer from the symptoms of schizophrenia usually are affected early in life, during adolescence or early adulthood. Because of this early onset, they miss out on many of the experiences of just growing up.

Mary became ill as a teenager, during her senior year in high school. She had her first break during the spring of that year. She hallucinated, heard voices, saw things, and had to be hospitalized.

After she was discharged from the hospital, she spent time around the house. She did not do much; often she was tired because of her medication. Naturally her family was concerned. They watched her closely after she was discharged. They knew she hallucinated and became psychotic when she was not on her medication, but now she seemed over-medicated.

That fall she tried to go to college without much success. She had to be hospitalized again. This story repeated itself for several years. Mary was in and out of the hospital several times.

Between hospitalizations Mary was not able to do much. She hung around the house; it was impossible for her to work, go to school or live independently. She had all the negative symptoms that seem to accompany schizophrenia. In her early twenties she got involved with our research program. She responded, but she had missed out on the process of growing up. She had to go back through that process; she had many things to learn. How does one "catch up" after suffering from a serious illness for five or six years? This process takes time and work, and yes, a program. Social skills have to be learned. Vocational skills have to be acquired. Everyday living must be experienced: getting an apartment, buying food, managing money. All these skills and others need to be learned if independent living is to be achieved.

Mary was involved in a program for over a year that helped her learn these skills. There were eight other patients in the program. They met together several times a week in various settings. Social skills were learned, as were skills of everyday living: how to make a budget, apply for a job, clean an apartment. The ultimate goal of this program was independent living.

Job skills are especially important. To be fully independent, one must enter the work force. This goal is often difficult. We were fortunate in Louisville; we had work opportunities for our patients. Several companies were sympathetic to the needs of our patients. They could gradually get back into the work force.

Re-entry takes time, effort, and hard work. Using new medications, such as Clozaril, and by trying current medications, such as lithium, Depakote, or Tegretol to see if there is a good response, many patients lose their negative symptoms and have an opportunity to re-enter society. They can learn job skills, social skills, and everyday living skills. We need more programs that focus on this area of treatment. Independent living is no longer a dream. For many it could be reality.

Income

Patients who suffer from bipolar illness or schizophrenia are often unable to work. This puts a great financial burden on families. There are services that can help in these cases: 1) Social Security Disability Insurance (SSDI) is for disabled workers who paid into the social security system when they worked. Payments are based on past earnings. A patient who becomes disabled before age twenty-two may collect SSDI under a parent's account if the parent is retired, disabled, or deceased. 2) Supplementary Security Income (SSI) provides help to those who are aged, blind, or disabled. SSI is based on need. Patients on SSI also qualify for Medicaid. 3) Food stamps are also available.

Social workers know about these services. They can be very helpful in guiding patients and families through the process of securing assistance through these programs.

The Family and Long-Term Support Systems

How do familes support loved ones over the long haul? Certainly with some difficulty and some agonizing questions. If families burn out, there is no replacement family. Plans need to be made that do not wear out family members or cause intolerable stress. Very few families can provide total care.

Families need to seek out agencies and programs in their communities that can be of help. Often parents are the care givers. But as care givers, parents and families need help. Agencies can provide help.

As a physician, I learned that if I worked too long and too hard, I would burn out. Medicine can be all consuming. I could not let this happen. I am glad I learned this early in my career.

Many professions and experiences in life can be all consuming. My experience has shown that what the families of patients with chronic mental illness face is often the most exhausting experience anyone can encounter. All one's physical and emotional resources are called upon daily. Parents need a break from the care of their loved one; in fact, they need frequent breaks to survive.

If you burn out, you cannot be replaced. Take time off; get relief. Do not feel guilty about it. Every family needs a life of its own. Family members deserve a respite. Find the help you need.

In most families other children will need you as well. Younger siblings are often overlooked when the pressures of caring for an ill son or daughter are all encompassing. The needs of all children require attention. Support groups can help with the complex family dilemmas and needs that arise. All children need to feel valued and loved. They need to feel wanted. Being overburdened makes these feelings difficult to address. Patients sometimes demand more care than anyone can give. This imbalance between what patients need and what families can give leads to feelings of anger, resentment, and guilt. These issues deserve careful thought and planning.

There's an old saying: To keep a lamp burning, you have to put fuel in it. A family is the lamp that guides us through darkness. Take time to find the fuel you need to keep going. This may mean going out to dinner, taking a walk, calling a friend, enrolling in a class, or taking up a hobby. Whatever interests and sustains you is time well spent — fuel added to the lamp.

20

Private vs. Public

Parents and family members want to provide the best care they can for their loved ones. Often what care is provided depends on finances. Families have financial limitations. Because of the chronicity of these illnesses, most families eventually run into financial problems. Often loved ones have come to me deeply distressed over these issues. They want the best for their family members, but they just do not have the money for private hospitalization or a private psychiatrist.

Private hospitalization does not always provide the best care available. I gave an example of a very prestigious private hospital that had a patient for thirty years who was not given medication and, essentially, remained psychotic. I have not been overly convinced that the private sector gives better care than the public sector. Often, the opposite is true. I know that I would not have allowed a psychotic person to remain off medication. I would have forced the issue some way. There are ways to do that.

One way is to get family members to help. They can persuade patients to take medication. At times, when we were treating very aggressive patients who would not take their medication we would call in several security guards. Their presence was very persuasive. Nurses are also helpful in getting patients to take medication.

The real issue here depends on the interpretation of these illnesses. If they are genetic and biochemical, then the basis of treatment centers around changing brain chemistry. This calls for medication as the foundation of treatment. If they are illnesses from a problem of family environment, then the foundation of treatment becomes psychotherapy of some sort. This is a basic, fundamental point. I recently had a discussion with the director of a community mental health center. I was upset with him because patients were taken off Clozaril when they came into the stabilization unit. They were never restarted on it. Patients were not put on Clozaril as outpatients, and the center did not use lithium, Depakote, or Tegretol either. My point with him was that without a good foundation using medication, no matter what other protocol was used, the treatment would not be effective. This treatment has to do with basic philosophy.

Another issue that influences treatment philosophy is the psychiatrist's attitude about the chronicity of these illnesses. When one has worked with chronic patients who rarely show improvement, one becomes discouraged and complacent. The psychiatrist does not expect much to work, and believes all medications to be the same — that it does not matter which medication is prescribed. This attitude just does not reflect what is possible. This attitude is just not correct. Ned's case was a good example that it is important what medications are used in treatment. Lithium turned around his life. I could cite many other examples like Ned's.

Treatment philosophy is such a critical issue. Find out about this illness. Study, read, ask questions. Join NAMI and the National Depressive and Manic-Depressive Association (NDMDA). Be informed. Develop a treatment philosophy. Find a psychiatrist with whom you agree, either in the private or public sector. There are good psychiatrists in both areas.

Good care is not always best when costs are high, or buildings and facilities are attractive. Good care depends on treatment philosophies and a knowledgeable, caring staff. Look for these qualities in community mental health centers. Evaluate private hospitals and universities' departments of psychiatry. Do not feel guilty about not being able to afford private care. The public sector also can provide good, competent care. Find the best care you can, under whatever circumstances you encounter.

One time I was asked, "Should I have my daughter hospitalized for six months so that she can get enough intense psychotherapy to figure this whole thing out?" This father was hoping that psychotherapy could unravel what was going on with his daughter and make her well again. This just does not happen. Psychotherapy cannot remove paranoid delusions or hallucinations; it just cannot. Yet often family members think it can. They search for the perfect psychotherapist who can get rid of symptoms. Psychotherapy does not get rid of the symptoms of schizophrenia.

The obvious question then is: Does psychotherapy help at all? In a classic study done several decades ago, Philip May divided hospitalized patients into five experimental treatment groups. Group 1 received medication; group 2 received medication plus psychotherapy; group 3 received psychotherapy; group 4 received electroconvulsive therapy (ECT); and group 5 received milieu treatment. This last group served as a control. The patients were involved in treatment for at least six months. Some were treated for a year. May demonstrated that medications proved to be the best treatment for these patients. ECT was the next effective treatment. Psychotherapy alone had no real advantage over milieu therapy. Psychotherapy plus medication was not really different than medication alone.

Lester Grinspoon also studied patients in one inpatient setting during the 1970s. This study demonstrated that patients relapsed when taken off medications even though psychotherapy continued. Gerard Hogarty and Nina Schooler demonstrated the same findings for outpatients. They divided their patients into four groups. The first group received medication; the second group received medication and psychotherapy; the third group, psychotherapy and a placebo; the fourth group, a placebo. The relapse rate was much higher in the groups receiving no medication.

The question of the helpfulness of psychotherapy is still not answered completely. In-depth psychotherapy that delves into childhood development and experiences is not helpful in treating these illnesses. This concept seems certain. One cannot eliminate these illnesses with psychotherapy, as proven in studies and experiments.

If patients are asked if psychotherapy is helpful, most of them say it is. Certainly group therapy helps patients socialize and understand their illnesses better. Family therapy can also be helpful with the everyday problems of living. Psychotherapy is especially beneficial in the rehabilitation process that helps patients re-enter society after successful biological treatment has taken place. Our patients in Louisville who responded to our research protocol were involved in this rehabilitation process. They had group therapy every week. They were also involved in other resocialization programs that helped the re-entry process. Patients have a lot to learn, a lot of questions to ask when the normal socialization process has been stopped or slowed down. Our patients needed these programs and were involved in them. Lithium responders, Depakote responders, Tegretol responders, Clozaril responders — all of these patients who are emerging from their chronic illnesses need this kind of program.

Again, the question: Is therapy helpful? The answer: Yes, it is. Therapy does not get rid of the chronic illnesses, but it does help patients re-enter society after successful response to medication. It also helps families cope with these illnesses more effectively.

21

Medications for the Future

Throughout previous chapters I have referred to the new medications available. These medications are of such significance that I want to devote this chapter to summarizing the important contributions they offer now and for the future.

Clozaril (generic name, clozapine) is an atypical antipsychotic agent that is distinctly different in its action when compared with the conventional antipsychotic medications that have been used since the 1950s. Clozaril is both chemically and pharmacologically different than other antipsychotic agents. It is thought to act on different receptor sites in the brain. It controls a broader spectrum of psychotic symptoms than does Thorazine, and Clozaril controls these symptoms more effectively. Numerous studies have shown that Clozaril works better than Thorazine or Haldol in the treatment of schizophrenia. You will find references of these studies included in the bibliography in the back of this book.

The side effects of Clozaril are also different than those of the more conventional antipsychotic medications. Clozaril causes almost no extrapyramidal side effects. Extrapyramidal side effects refer to a range of neurological side effects including muscle spasms, stiffness of joints, shaking movements of extremities. Clozaril does not cause these extrapyramidal side effects.

Clozaril also does not cause tardive dyskinesia. Tardive dyskinesia is another extrapyramidal side effect that is associated with the more conventional antipsychotic medications. Tardive dyskinesia refers to abnormal, involuntary, irregular movements usually involving the face, mouth, tongue, neck, arms and legs. The tongue is overactive; it protrudes from the mouth or darts in and out of the mouth. The lips appear puckered. The face grimaces and the jaw has lateral movements. These effects are most evident and troublesome in older patients who have been on antipsychotic medications for quite some time. The incidence is 2 to 7 percent over the first seven years on medication, and as high as 50 to 70 percent in chronically hospitalized patients.

Tardive dyskinesia is difficult to treat. Even when the conventional antipsychotic medication is discontinued, the tardive dyskinesia often does not subside. Let me repeat: Clozaril does not have this side effect, and in fact Clozaril is often given to patients who may have developed this side effect when taking conventional antipsychotic medications. Patients maintained on Clozaril do not develop tardive dyskinesia.

Another interesting feature of Clozaril is that it does not increase prolactin levels in the serum. This means that female patients do not experience a disruption in their menstrual cycles; they also do not experience enlarged breasts or secretions from their breasts that may occur when prolactin levels increase.

Though Clozaril does not cause the bothersome side effects described, there are side effects to Clozaril. Patients may experience mild tremors, akathisia (restlessness, constant motion, a condition in which a patient feels unable to remain still) and occasional muscle rigidity. There is an increased risk of seizures; up to 2 percent of patients have seizures when the dose is above 300 milligrams/day. This risk climbs to 5 percent when the dose exceeds 600 milligrams/day. Patients are monitored for this side effect and can be treated effectively if seizures occur.

Another side effect of Clozaril is agranulocytosis, bone marrow suppression. The incidence of this is in the range of 3 percent. Agranulocytosis is a serious side effect that can be fatal. But it can be prevented by monitoring patients' white blood cell count. This monitoring is done by weekly laboratory tests conducted on small amounts of blood drawn from the patient. If the white blood cell count falls below three thousand, Clozaril is discontinued. The risk of agranulocytosis is why Clozaril is dispensed on a weekly basis. The week's prescription for medication is not given to the patient until after the white blood cell count has been checked. This system of monitoring effectively prevents agranulocytosis.

The risks of any medication must be balanced against the advantages. Agranulocytosis is a risk of Clozaril, but a preventable risk when weekly white blood cell counts are monitored. This monitoring, however, means having blood drawn every week — a difficult and unpleasant task to endure each week. No one likes to have blood drawn. Patients, also, must be seen each week to be evaluated. Again, inconvenient. Another drawback is it costs a lot to be evaluated and monitored every week. In some states, however, Medicaid will pay for the blood tests because patients on Clozaril do not need hospitalization as often as other patients, and thus the cost of care is reduced.

The strongest advantage of Clozaril is that patients feel better. They do not have a lot of bothersome side effects to endure. They are more motivated, more alert and active. Compliance is not a great problem; patients are willing to stay on the medication because they do not have the bothersome side effects. When patients stay on their medication, they generally do not decompensate or become psychotic as often.

From my point of view, the reason Clozaril is a major breakthrough in the treatment of schizophrenia is not its lack of side effects, but rather the broad spectrum of symptoms it treats. The main drawback of the conventional antipsychotic medications has been their ineffectiveness with the so-called negative symptoms of schizophrenia. These conventional medications are very good at treating the acute phase of the illness. A psychiatrist usually can get patients out of an acute psychotic episode with these medications. These medications also prevent the recurrence of the acute phase of the illness, and thus, keep patients out of the hospital. But the conventional ones are not effective in treating the negative symptoms of schizophrenia. These are the symptoms that lead to the personality deterioration that is so common among these patients. These are the symptoms that make life so difficult for these patients. They have a hard time concentrating, getting motivated or getting started to do things; they have a hard time working, going to school or living independently.

To differentiate between positive and negative symptoms, consider the notion of adding and taking away. Positive symptoms involve thoughts and behaviors that are not present in normal functioning, but are present in persons suffering from the symptoms of schizophrenia, such as auditory hallucinations and paranoid delusions. By contrast, negative refers to something reduced or taken away. Negative symptoms are behaviors present in normal functioning, but are not present in patients suffering from the symptoms of schizophrenia. When patients do not have or lose the ability to concentrate or become motivated, they are experiencing negative symptoms. That means they have less than what is considered normal functioning, a taking away, a negative.

In multiple studies in the United States and Europe involving over seven hundred fifty patients, Clozaril proved to be superior to Haldol and Thorazine across the spectrum of positive and negative symptoms. Clozaril is a breakthrough medication in the treatment of schizophrenia; with this medication patients can experience a future of greater hope and possibility, with greater control of both positive and negative symptoms.

Risperdal (generic name, risperidone) is another new medication. It has been tested extensively in the United States and Canada. A recent article presented in the May, 1995, *Psychiatric Annals* reports that eight weeks of treatment on Risperdal 6 milligrams/day was superior to Haldol in the total positive and negative syndrome scale. The important finding was that negative symptoms were significantly reduced with Risperdal. As mentioned before, these are the symptoms that are not responsive to conventional antipsychotics.

Studies from both the United States and Canada have been presented to the Food and Drug Administration as a single data set. Haldol 20 milligrams/day was clearly less effective than Risperdal 6 milligrams/day on positive, negative and global measures. The international study showed that Risperdal was also superior to conventional antipsychotics. These studies demonstrated that extrapyramidal side effects were the same as those experienced by patients on placebo medication; that means patients on Risperdal did not experience extrapyramidal side effects any more than patients receiving placebo medications. The rate of tardive dyskinesia is also reduced. Sedation is the most common side effect reported with Risperdal.

Patients can be started on Risperdal at any time. Clozaril, on the other hand, is reserved for refractory patients, patients who do not respond to conventional medications, and patients with movement disorder side effects. Another advantage of Risperdal is that weekly blood tests are not required.

Zyprexa (generic name, olanzapine) is an atypical antipsychotic medication that has been developed by the Eli Lilly Pharmaceutical Company. The hope is that Zyprexa would have the benefits of Clozaril, that is, it would not only treat the patient's symptoms of schizophrenia but the negative ones as well without the bone marrow suppression that is seen in 3 percent of patients on Clozaril. In a double blind study, Zyprexa was compared to Haloperidol, a conventional neuroleptic. Patients were divided into two groups. One group received Haloperidol and the other group received Zyprexa. More patients prematurely left the Haloperidol group than the Zyprexa group. This means that the side effects of Haloperidol were more annoying than the side effects of Zyprexa. Positive symptom improvement and negative symptom improvement were better in the group of patients who were on Zyprexa. Patient compliance to medication and quality of life improvement scores were also better in patients receiving Zyprexa.

Tardive dyskinesia, Parkinsonism and akathesia were manifested less often in the Zyprexa group of patients. As yet, bone marrow suppression has not been a problem with patients on Zyprexa.

Zyprexa could well be a very good antipsychotic medication that offers new hope to patients. It has been released for use this October, 1996.

About six months ago, Jack walked into my office with his wife and little boy. He was obviously very disturbed. He was not sleeping at night, and he was so paranoid that he could not look at me. He also heard voices and was delusional. Jack was acutely psychotic. I prescribed Thorazine, gradually working to a dose of 1200 mg a day. Although this medication had very little effect on him for the first month, eventually his paranoia responded. He could talk to me and felt more comfortable in my office. Overall, however, little had changed. After about five months of very little improvement, Jack was started on Eli Lilly's new atypical antipsychotic, Zyprexa, which was just released. I added 10 mg of it to the Thorazine that Jack was already taking. After one week, Jack was sleeping more during the night. His affect was not as blunted and he was not as paranoid. His voices were not as intense either. I was able to reduce his Thorazine to 800 mg. The next week he showed more improvement. He smiled, related better, and was even less paranoid. I was very impressed with how Zyprexa improved Jack's condition. He was a lot better. I admit that one patient over a two-week period does not prove much, but I was really encouraged by what I saw. I hope that Jack continues to improve. I feel that Zyprexa may be a very useful medication in the treatment of schizophrenia.

New developments in psychopharmacology are also occurring in the treatment of bipolar disorder. Clozaril has been effective in patients suffering from the symptoms of bipolar disorder. That is good news.

In addition, Depakote and Tegretol, medications that have been used successfully in the treatment of seizure disorders, have also been effective in the treatment of bipolar disorder. We know that Depakote can smooth out the highs and lows of bipolar disorder. So can Tegretol. When patients do not respond to lithium, these medications provide alternatives. They are more effective in the treatment of rapid cycling patients and patients who show dysphoric mania. These medications are now first choice medications when these symptoms are present.

Depakote and Tegretol also work in combination with each other. Lithium and Depakote or lithium and Tegretol may work in combination when lithium alone is ineffective. In some cases, all three medications in combination may prove effective in patients non-responsive to single or dual medication regimens. These combinations give us more alternatives to try with treatment resistant patients. This is good news, indeed.

At this time new atypical antipsychotics are being produced and tested, and older medications are being used in new ways. These alternatives bring great hope to families and patients. Improved drugs herald a new era in psychopharmacology for patients suffering from the symptoms of schizophrenia, schizoaffective illness and bipolar illness. The goal of these treatments is to expand possibilities and enhance the lives of patients and their families. These medications can help patients live more normal lives, hold down jobs, go to school if they want, and live more independently. With these and future advancements in treatment options, such possibilities can become realities in the lives of patients and their families.

22
Hope for the Future

As I began to write the closing chapter for this book, I found myself confronted with a question: What can be the end to a book such as this, a book for patients and families living with chronic illness? The only words that seemed to answer that question were words of hope — hope for new discoveries, new insights, new diagnostic tools, new treatments — hope for the future. I have seen this hope realized in the lives of patients who have been described in the preceding chapters.

In chapter one I discussed the turmoil and loss experienced by Ned and his family. Ned came for an appointment recently; he is a student at the University of North Florida now. He is able to work and go to school. At this time, no signs exist of the illness that plagued him for seven years. Ned takes his medications every day. He knows how important this regimen is for him. So far none of the symptoms that Ned lived with for seven long years have broken through. At this point in time, Ned is symptom-free. Cured? I wouldn't say that, but he certainly lives a symptom-free life. He can do anything with his capabilities; he lives a normal existence. Sure, he has to take lithium; he has to have occasional blood tests; he has outpatient appointments every month. But he is symptom-free.

Ned and many patients like him, patients who are now symptom-free, bring hope to us all — hope for our sons and daughters, our loved ones, our friends. These patients also bring hope to me as I work and struggle with chronic illnesses in the lives of my patients and their families. Lives can be reclaimed. The future is not hopeless.

These patients' experiences do not need to be isolated ones. New discoveries, new insights, new diagnostic tools, new treatments are being discovered almost every day. I have just been to a conference that brought together scientists from the National Institute of Mental Health, universities and the pharmaceutical industry. New developments are happening all the time. I was encouraged by the findings reported at the conference. Every day we understand the physiology of the brain better than we once did. We know more about how and why medications work. More is understood about the relationship of diagnosis and treatment. I came away from the conference with renewed hope. But we need to know more. Research needs to be funded; studies need to be supported.

All of us can be part of these developments. We need to be involved with the National Alliance for the Mentally Ill and the National Depressive and Manic-Depressive Association. Collective voices are so much stronger than a voice spoken alone. Join these organizations; they too offer hope for the future.

The task ahead is formidable, but not impossible. Definitely not impossible. Have courage, and above all, do not give up hope. One day, we will understand these illnesses. One day, the lives of our loved ones will be turned around with new possibilities. And our hopes for the future will be realized, one day.

Epilogue

Schizophrenia is our most serious mental illness. One percent of the population suffers from it. As a society, the United States bears a heavy toll brought on by this illness — a toll measured in the cost of treatment and in the loss of productive contributions by patients and family members who live with schizophrenia. However, I believe the greatest cost is the failure that we as a society permit if we neglect the research needed to understand further this illness and minimize the burdens it imposes.

The problems of schizophrenia are complex ones which cannot be solved without research. Yet every year grants to study the disease become harder to obtain. The current allocation of funding is very competitive with countless obstacles for a research team. These obstacles keep the progress of research on an uncertain course. This course is a frustrating one for research teams who need stability and longevity in order to reach sustainable results of benefit to patients and society.

On one level the solution seems simple: recruit the most gifted, committed research professionals and provide them with a supportive atmosphere for their work. This solution, however, goes much deeper than mere recruitment and support. The critical issues are political, involving priorities that we as a society value and for which we are willing to dedicate our efforts. One of the most important steps we can all take is to join The National Alliance for the Mentally Ill (NAMI) and The National Depressive and Manic-Depressive Association (NDMDA). We also need to be members of local organizations that work on behalf of the mentally ill. Through membership in these organizations, our voice grows stronger and we can make a political impact. Several years ago I was able to get congressional support for research in schizophrenia. At that time I was told that to be really successful at raising money for research from Congress, one would need supporters and a political base. NAMI and NDMDA provide that base. We all need to be as active as possible in these and other organizations.

Another critical issue for the future is the support and leadership provided to the public sector for mental health care. We need more psychiatrists who are willing to face the challenges of working in the public health sector. At the present time, many psychiatrists leave or never enter this sector. When I was working in community mental health, I saw many highly qualified psychiatrists leave due to frustration from the overwhelming struggles they experienced each day. Unfortunately after many years in the public sector, I too left. My heart was there, but the obstacles became too great.

The reasons psychiatrists leave the public sector are many and varied, but one of the primary issues is the ongoing power and control conflicts that arise regarding professional decisions. These issues are complex and beyond the scope of this book, but they are of significance to all of us who care about the future directions of mental health services. As a society we cannot afford to turn our backs on the public sector of services. We need psychiatrists in private practice, but we also need to recruit and sustain the services of professionals who bring quality to public sectors.

One avenue to achieve this quality is to connect community mental health agencies and state hospitals to the departments of psychiatry of medical schools. More psychiatrists would be willing to come into a system under this auspices, and the quality of care would improve by recruiting and retaining professionals committed to both patients and leadership.

The departments of psychiatry at most medical schools are very biologically oriented. This means that they see genetic influences as being the key factor in the etiology of mental illness. Genetic factors show themselves in abnormal brain chemistry. To treat these illnesses, one must change brain chemistry with medication.

Some health care professionals would challenge this model. Despite more and more evidence pointing to the biological basis of schizophrenia, the debate continues with two opposing schools of thoughts, i.e., nature vs. nurture. Members of the latter group would be hesitant to encourage an increased emphasis on medications as the major treatment modality for this illness. But a shift of this nature is vital if we are going to address the biological factors of this disease. As discussed in the chapter on etiology, patients with schizophrenia suffer from an alteration in their brain chemistry. Only psychiatrists are trained and licensed to prescribe medications that can effectively change brain chemistry.

If all health care professionals can work together for the good of the patient, they can achieve advances in care that will offer hope to the many patients and families who live with this illness. Signs of hope are increasing. Sooner than we once expected, we will have laboratory tests, such as blood and urine evaluations, that will enable us to diagnose more accurately. Through genetic research we are closer to understanding which gene is responsible for schizophrenia. Newer, more effective medications are being produced, such as Clozaril, that offer real promise in treatment. Over time we are discovering more effective ways of using the medications we have been prescribing. Lithium, for example, is being used more frequently in treating these illnesses. We are finding more patients who respond to lithium. Patients who respond can live better lives. They can go to school, work, and live more independently. Furthermore, social workers, psychologists, and psychiatric nurses are playing vital roles in the resocialization of patients and counseling for families. We need to continue these advances through the grassroots efforts and national political arenas that influence research and funding. Whether personally or as members of society, all human beings are affected by these mental health issues.

Schizophrenia is coming out of the back wards and closets of ignorance that once brought much despair. Information leads to knowledge; knowledge removes the stigmas of the past, and in their place, we can promote awareness and understanding. The present and future are new eras, exciting eras, ones of challenge and hope.

Chapter Notes

Chapter 1: There is Hope
1. H.G. Pope, Jr., M.D. and J.F. Lipinski, Jr., M.D., "Diagnosis in Schizophrenia and Manic-Depressive Illness: A Reassessment of the Specificity of 'Schizophrenic' Symptoms in the Light of Current Research." *Archives of General Psychiatry* 35:7 (July 1978): 811-828.

Chapter 2: Etiology: How Do We Get These Illnesses?
1. David Rosenthal, Ph.D., Paul H. Wender, M.D., Seymour S. Kety, M.D., Joseph Welner, M.D., and Fini Schulsinger, M.D., "The Adopted-Away Offsprings of Schizophrenics," *American Journal of Psychiatry* 128:3 (September 1971).

2. Leonard L. Heston, "Psychiatric Disorders in Foster Home Reared Children of Schizophrenic Mothers," *British Journal of Psychiatry* 112 (1966): 819-825.

3. Margit Fischer, M.D., "Psychoses in the Offspring of Schizophrenic Monozygotic Twins and Their Normal Co-Twins, *British Journal of Psychiatry* 118 (1971): 43-52.

Chapter 3: Diagnosing: How Can We Do This Accurately?
1. Jonathan Cole, M.D. and Leo Hollister, M.D., *Schizophrenia* MedCom (1970).

2. H.G. Pope, Jr., M.D. and J.F. Lipinski, Jr., M.D., "Diagnosis in Schizophrenia and Manic-Depressive Illness: A Reassessment of the Specificity of 'Schizophrenic' Symptoms in the Light of Current Research." *Archives of General Psychiatry* 35:7 (July 1978): 811-828.

Chapter 4: Treatment: What Options are There?
1. Alen F. Schatzberg, M.D. and Jonathan O. Cole, M.D., *Manual of Clinical Psychopharmacology*, (Washington, D.C.: American Psychiatric Press, Inc., 1991).

2. Lester Grinspoon, M.D., Jack R. Ewalt, M.D., and Richard I. Shader, M.D., *Schizophrenia, Pharmacotherapy and Psychotherapy*, (Baltimore: The Williams and Williams Company, 1972).

3. Philip R.A. May, M.D., *Treatment of Schizophrenia*, (New York: Science House, 1968).

4. G.E. Hogarty, M.S.W., S.C. Goldberg, Ph.D., and N.R. Schooler, Ph.D., "Drug and Sociotherapy in the Aftercare of Schizophrenic Patients." *Archives of General Psychiatry* (November, 1974): 31: 603-608.

Chapter 6: Bipolar Disorder: A Case Study
1. Jonathan Cole, M.D. and Leo Hollister, M.D., *Schizophrenia* MedCom (1970).

2. Charles B. Nemeroff, M.D., Ph.D. and Robert M. Post, M.D., *Bipolar Disorder: Current Progress and Future Directions in Diagnosing and Management*, (Symposium: Amelia Island, Florida, September 27-30, 1992).

Chapter 7: Treatment: Options in Bipolar Disorders
1. Charles B. Nemeroff, M.D., Ph.D. and Robert M. Post, M.D., *Bipolar Disorder: Current Progress and Future Directions in Diagnosing and Management*, (Symposium: Amelia Island, Florida, September 27-30, 1992).

Chapter 8: Alternative Treatments for Bipolar Disorder
1. Charles B. Nemeroff, M.D., Ph.D. and Robert M. Post, M.D., *Bipolar Disorder: Current Progress and Future Directions in Diagnosing and Management*, (Symposium: Amelia Island, Florida, September 27-30, 1992).

Chapter 9: Depression: A Treatment Dilemma
1. Charles B. Nemeroff, M.D., Ph.D. and Robert M. Post, M.D., *Bipolar Disorder: Current Progress and Future Directions in Diagnosing and Management,* (Symposium: Amelia Island, Florida, September 27-30, 1992).

Chapter 10: Schizoaffective Disorder
1. Jonathan Cole, M.D. and Leo Hollister, M.D., *Schizophrenia* MedCom (1970).

2. Charles B. Nemeroff, M.D., Ph.D. and Robert M. Post, M.D., *Bipolar Disorder: Current Progress and Future Directions in Diagnosing and Management,* (Symposium: Amelia Island, Florida, September 27-30, 1992).

Chapter 11: Issues of Living
1. Agnes B. Hartfield, Ph.D., *Coping with Mental Illness in the Family,* NAMI Book no. 6, (July, 1991).

2. Carol M. Anderson, Douglas J. Reiss, and Gerard E. Hogarty, *Schizophrenia and the Family,* The Guilford Press, New York, London (1986).

Chapter 12: Coping with Mental Illness in the Family
1. Agnes B. Hartfield, Ph.D., *Coping with Mental Illness in the Family,* NAMI Book no. 6, (July, 1991).

Chapter 13: Choosing Treatment
1. E. Fuller Torrey, M.D., *Surviving Schizophrenia: A Family Manual,* (New York: Harper and Row, 1983).

Chapter 17: Problem Solving, Setting Limits
1. Agnes B. Hartfield, Ph.D., *Coping with Mental Illness in the Family,* NAMI Book no. 6, (July, 1991).

Chapter 21: Medications for the Future
1. Edited by Jerome Yesavage, M.D., *Clozapine: A Compendium of Selected Readings, 3rd edition,* (Stanford, California: Sandos Pharmaceutical Corporation, 1994).

Bibliography

Anderson, Carol, et al. *Schizophrenia and the Family.*

Cole, Jonathan, M.D. and Leo Hollister. *Schizophrenia.* MedCom, 1970.

Cole, Jonathan O., M.D., editor. *Psychopharmacology Update.* Lexington, Massachusetts, Toronto: The Callamore Press D.C. Health and Company, 1980.

Grinspoon, Lester, M.D., et al. *Schizophrenia, Pharmacotherapy and Psychotherapy.* Baltimore: The Williams and Williams Company, 1972.

Hartfield, Agnes B., Ph.D. *Coping with Mental Illness in the Family.* NAMI Book no. 6.

Hogarty, G.E., and S.C. Goldberg, et al. "Drug and Sociotherapy in Aftercare of Schizophrenic Patients, II: Two-Year Relapse Rates." *Archives of General Psychiatry.* 1974: Volume 31. 603-608.

May, Philip, M.D. *Treatment of Schizophrenia.* New York: Science House, 1968.

Nemeroff, Charles B., M.D., Ph.D. and Robert M. Post, M.D. *Bipolar Disorder: Current Progress and Future Directions in Diagnosing and Management.* Amelia Island, Florida, 1992.

Pope, H.G., Jr., M.D. and J.F. Lipinski, Jr., M.D. "Diagnosis in Schizophrenia and Manic-Depressive Illness: A Reassessment of the Specificity of 'Schizophrenic' Symptoms in the Light of Current Research." *Archives of General Psychiatry.* July 1978: 811-828.

Post, Robert M., M.D. and James C. Ballenger, M.D., editors. *Neurobiology of Mood Disorders.* Baltimore/London: Williams and Wilkins, 1984.

Rosenthal, David, Ph.D., et al. "The Adopted-Away Offsprings of Schizophrenics." *American Journal of Psychiatry.* September 1971.

Schatzberg, Alen F., M.D. and Jonathan O. Cole, M.D. *Manual of Clinical Psychopharmacology.* Washington, D.C.: American Psychiatric Press, Inc., 1991.

Torrey, E. Fuller, M.D. *Surviving Schizophrenia: A Family Manual.* New York: Harper and Row, 1983.

Yesavage, Jerome, M.D., ed. *Clozapine: A Compendium of Selected Readings, 3rd edition.* Sandos Pharmaceutical Corporation, 1994.

Recommended Reading

Balter, Marie and Richard Katz. *Nobody's Child*. Menlo Park: Merloyd Books, 1991.

Devson, Anne. *Tell Me I'm Here: One Family's Experience of Schizophrenia*. Introduction by E. Fuller Torrey, M.D. New York: Penguin Books, 1992.

Gottesman, Irving I. *Schizophrenia Genesis: The Origins of Madness*. New York: W.H. Freeman and Co., 1991.

Hales, Dianne and Robert Hales. *Caring for the Mind: The Comprehensive Guide to Mental Health*. New York: Bantam Books, 1995.

Heston, Leonard L. *Mending Minds*. New York: W.H. Freeman and Co., 1992.

Spar, James and Asenath LaRue. *Geriatric Psychiatry*. Washington, D.C.: American Psychiatric Press, 1990.

Torrey, E. Fuller, Ann E. Bowler, Edward H. Taylor and Irving I. Gottesman. *Schizophrenia and Manic-Depressive Disorder*. New York: Basic Books, 1994.

Torrey, E. Fuller. *Surviving Schizophrenia: A Family Manual*. (rev. ed.). New York: Harper & Row, 1988.

Wagemaker, Herbert. *The Surprising Truth About Depression*. Grand Rapids: Zondervan Publishing House, 1994.

Woolis, Rebecca. *When Someone You Love Has A Mental Illness*. New York: G.P. Putnam's Sons, 1992.

Appendix

American Psychiatric Association
    1400 K Street, N.W.
    Washington, D.C. 20005
    (202) 682-6000 or (202) 682-6220

National Alliance for the Mentally Ill
    200 North Glebe Road
    Suite 1015
    Arlington, VA 22203
    (703) 524-7600 or (800) 950-6264

National Depressive and Manic-Depressive Association
    730 North Franklin Street
    Suite 501
    Chicago, IL 60610
    (312) 642-0049 or (800) 82-NDMDA

National Institute of Mental Health Public Information
    5600 Fishers Lane
    Room 7-99
    Rockville, MD 20857
    (301) 443-4536 or (800) 421-4211

National Mental Health Association
    1021 Prince Street
    Alexandria, VA 22314-2971
    (703) 684-7722 or (800) 969-NMHA

Algorithms for Treating the Acute Phase of Schizophrenia,
Bipolar Disorder, or Schizoaffective Illness

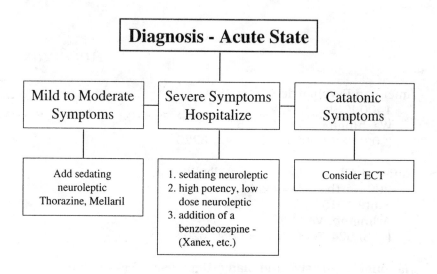

Algorithms for Treating the Post-Acute Phase of
Schizophrenia, Bipolar Disorder, or Schizoaffective Illness

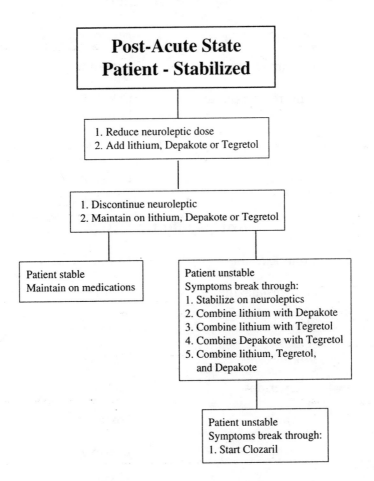

**Post-Acute State
Patient - Stabilized**

1. Reduce neuroleptic dose
2. Add lithium, Depakote or Tegretol

1. Discontinue neuroleptic
2. Maintain on lithium, Depakote or Tegretol

Patient stable
Maintain on medications

Patient unstable
Symptoms break through:
1. Stabilize on neuroleptics
2. Combine lithium with Depakote
3. Combine lithium with Tegretol
4. Combine Depakote with Tegretol
5. Combine lithium, Tegretol,
   and Depakote

Patient unstable
Symptoms break through:
1. Start Clozaril

Mood Stabilizers

Generic Name	*Brand Name*
carbamazepine	Tegretol
lithium carbonate	Eskalith Lithane Lithotabs Lithobid
valproate	Depakote

Antipsychotic Drugs

Generic Name	*Brand Name*
chlorpromazine	Thorazine
clozapine	Clozaril
fluphenazine	Prolixin
haloperidol	Haldol
loxapine	Loxitane
olanzapine	Zyprexa
perphenazine	Trilafon
risperidone	Risperdal
thioridazine	Mellaril
thiothixene	Navane
trifluoperazine	Stelazine

Glossary

Acute psychotic state: Lack of sleep, excitement, hallucinations, delusions, out of touch with reality — patients often need to be hospitalized in this state. They can be dangerous to themselves and others.

Affect: Another term for moods. Patients suffering from schizophrenia have blunted or flat affects. Patients suffering from bipolar disorder often show manic affect.

Affect disorder: These disorders are mood or affect disorders and include depression, bipolar disorder, schizoaffective disorder and alcoholism.

Agranulocytosis: Suppression of bone marrow that can be fatal. White blood cell counts fall and patients are susceptible to infection.

Atypical Neuroleptic: A medication, like Clozaril, that acts differently in the brain than conventional neuroleptics and has different effects in patients. Clozaril, for example, treats negative as well as positive symptoms in patients suffering from schizophrenia.

Catatonic: Patients with a down, unresponsive state.

Delusions: False beliefs that are so ingrained in a person that one cannot talk the person out of them.

Double bind theory: A theory that states schizophrenia is caused by families that put their children in impossible situations and give them options that don't work — a damned if you do, damned if you do not situation. This theory is not held by many in the field today.

Etiology: The cause of an illness. In the case of schizophrenia and bipolar disorder the etiology is genetic and shows itself in abnormal brain chemistry.

Euphoria: Grandiose, manic moods, usually found in patients suffering from bipolar disorder.

Family history of illness: Are there any family members that have illnesses that are similar to the patient's? We look for evidence of schizophrenia, bipolar disorder, depression, alcoholism. Families that have affective disorders tend to produce members that have affective disorders. Families that have members with schizophrenia tend to produce members that have schizophrenia.

Lithium: A naturally-occurring salt that has been very useful in treating bipolar disorders and schizoaffective disorders, as well as some patients diagnosed as suffering from symptoms of schizophrenia.

Major tranquilizers: Another name for antipsychotic medications. These medications do more than tranquilize, they also treat psychotic features of an illness.

Natural history of illness: How an illness manifests itself over the life of the patient. This manifestation often gives a clue to diagnosis and is important in separating patients who suffer from schizophrenia from patients who suffer from bipolar disorders.

Negative symptoms: Withdrawal, blunted affect, lack of motivation, unable to finish tasks — symptoms that prevent patients from living independently, working, going to school, doing the things that enable people to live in society.

Neologisms: The manufacture of new words that are then incorporated into a patient's language.

Neuroleptics: Antipsychotic medications used to stabilize patients, to bring them out of an acute psychotic state, and to control the symptoms of schizophrenia or bipolar disorder.

Paranoia: The delusion that people are watching you, out to get you, trying to hurt you.

Perception: Seeing things, hearing things, feeling things, smelling things, when nothing is there. Common in patients suffering from schizophrenia and also in patients suffering from bipolar disorders.

Personality deterioration: The inability to work, to attend school, to live independently, that is present in patients suffering from schizophrenia.

Post-acute state: The state that follows the acute psychotic state, when a patient has been stabilized. At this period of time, the treatment goals change to finding a medication that will treat negative symptoms and allow a patient to be involved in the re-entry process.

Presenting symptoms: These are the symptoms a patient has that give you the idea that something is going on. In the acute psychotic state, these symptoms include hallucinations, delusions, feeling paranoid, excitement, mania, or problems sleeping.

Pressured speech: The rapid speech that is so common in patients suffering from mania.

Psychomotor retardation: The slowing down of thinking, talking, walking, etc. Everything just slows down.

Re-entry: The process of relearning the skills needed in working, finding friends, living independently and getting back into the mainstream of society.

Refractory patients: Patients who have not responded to the medication such that they still exhibit symptoms of the illness.

Schizoaffective disorder: An illness that has the characteristics of schizophrenia and bipolar disorders. It falls somewhere between them. Patients suffering from this disorder may respond to lithium or to the anticonvulsant medications.

Schizophrenogenic mother: A mother who was thought to cause schizophrenia in a child. This theory is no longer believed, but the influence still lingers in some circles.

Stabilization: When patients do not exhibit the symptoms of the acute psychotic state — they are stabilized on their medication.

Thought disorder: Another name for schizophrenia. Schizophrenia is a disorder of thinking. Patients often feel that thoughts and/or feelings are inserted into their minds. They also feel that their thoughts are being controlled by outside forces.

Vegetative state: Patients are withdrawn, isolated, with no motivation and blunted, flat affects. This state is found in patients suffering from the side effects of the medication used with schizophrenia. These are the effects of medications that are often not helpful to patients. Every medication has side effects. Usually, the positive effects of medication offset the negative side effects. Only occasionally do side effects cause a discontinuation of a medication.

Index

Order Form
Publications & Videotapes by Herbert Wagemaker, M.D.

TITLE (Softcover Books)	Quantity	Cost	Total Cost
The Surprising Truth About Depression		$10 ea.	
Schizophrenia and Bipolar Disorders — often misdiagnosed, often mistreated: A Family Manual		$12 ea.	
VIDEOTAPE TITLE	**Quantity**	**Cost**	**Total Cost**
Schizophrenia		$10 ea.	
Bipolar Disorder		$10 ea.	
Depression		$10 ea.	
Adolescent Depression & Suicide		$10 ea.	
Postpartum Depression		$10 ea.	
Panic Disorder		$10 ea.	
Obsessive Compulsive Disorder		$10 ea.	
Attention Deficit Disorder & Hyperactivity		$10 ea.	
Learning Tapes - make learning fun/productive 1. elementary child 2. middle school age 3. high school age		$10 ea. $10 ea. $10 ea.	
Florida Residents add 6 1/2% for Sales Tax			
Shipping & Handling: $2/book & $2.50/videotape			
Total Amount Paid			

Shipping Address:
Name: _____
Address: _____
City: _____ State: _____ Zip: _____

Make checks payable to: **Ponte Vedra Publishers,**
P.O. Box 773, Ponte Vedra Beach, FL 32004-0773
Please allow 3 – 4 weeks for delivery.

Order Form
Publications & Videotapes by Herbert Wagemaker, M.D.

TITLE (Softcover Books)	Quantity	Cost	Total Cost
The Surprising Truth About Depression		$10 ea.	
Schizophrenia and Bipolar Disorders — often misdiagnosed, often mistreated: A Family Manual		$12 ea.	
VIDEOTAPE TITLE	**Quantity**	**Cost**	**Total Cost**
Schizophrenia		$10 ea.	
Bipolar Disorder		$10 ea.	
Depression		$10 ea.	
Adolescent Depression & Suicide		$10 ea.	
Postpartum Depression		$10 ea.	
Panic Disorder		$10 ea.	
Obsessive Compulsive Disorder		$10 ea.	
Attention Deficit Disorder & Hyperactivity		$10 ea.	
Learning Tapes - make learning fun/productive 1. elementary child 2. middle school age 3. high school age		$10 ea. $10 ea. $10 ea.	
Florida Residents add 6 1/2% for Sales Tax			
Shipping & Handling: $2/book & $2.50/videotape			
Total Amount Paid			

Shipping Address:
Name: _____
Address: _____
City: _____ State: _____ Zip: _____

Make checks payable to: **Ponte Vedra Publishers,
P.O. Box 773, Ponte Vedra Beach, FL 32004-0773**
Please allow 3 – 4 weeks for delivery.

Order Form

Publications & Videotapes by Herbert Wagemaker, M.D.

TITLE (Softcover Books)	Quantity	Cost	Total Cost
The Surprising Truth About Depression		$10 ea.	
Schizophrenia and Bipolar Disorders — often misdiagnosed, often mistreated: A Family Manual		$12 ea.	

VIDEOTAPE TITLE	Quantity	Cost	Total Cost
Schizophrenia		$10 ea.	
Bipolar Disorder		$10 ea.	
Depression		$10 ea.	
Adolescent Depression & Suicide		$10 ea.	
Postpartum Depression		$10 ea.	
Panic Disorder		$10 ea.	
Obsessive Compulsive Disorder		$10 ea.	
Attention Deficit Disorder & Hyperactivity		$10 ea.	
Learning Tapes - make learning fun/productive 1. elementary child 2. middle school age 3. high school age		$10 ea. $10 ea. $10 ea.	
Florida Residents add 6 1/2% for Sales Tax			
Shipping & Handling: $2/book & $2.50/videotape			
Total Amount Paid			

Shipping Address:
Name: _____
Address: _____
City: _____ State: _____ Zip: _____

Make checks payable to: **Ponte Vedra Publishers,
P.O. Box 773, Ponte Vedra Beach, FL 32004-0773**
Please allow 3 – 4 weeks for delivery.

Order Form
Publications & Videotapes by Herbert Wagemaker, M.D.

TITLE (Softcover Books)	Quantity	Cost	Total Cost
The Surprising Truth About Depression		$10 ea.	
Schizophrenia and Bipolar Disorders — often misdiagnosed, often mistreated: A Family Manual		$12 ea.	
VIDEOTAPE TITLE	**Quantity**	**Cost**	**Total Cost**
Schizophrenia		$10 ea.	
Bipolar Disorder		$10 ea.	
Depression		$10 ea.	
Adolescent Depression & Suicide		$10 ea.	
Postpartum Depression		$10 ea.	
Panic Disorder		$10 ea.	
Obsessive Compulsive Disorder		$10 ea.	
Attention Deficit Disorder & Hyperactivity		$10 ea.	
Learning Tapes - make learning fun/productive 1. elementary child 2. middle school age 3. high school age		$10 ea. $10 ea. $10 ea.	
Florida Residents add 6 1/2% for Sales Tax			
Shipping & Handling: $2/book & $2.50/videotape			
Total Amount Paid			

Shipping Address:
Name: _____
Address: _____
City: _____ State: _____ Zip: _____

Make checks payable to: **Ponte Vedra Publishers,
P.O. Box 773, Ponte Vedra Beach, FL 32004-0773**
Please allow 3 – 4 weeks for delivery.